The Lakehouse Confession

By

Ashley Dawson

Dedication

To my sister Vidwaty Juliette R. Thank you for all your kindness extended to my family and me. Most of all Thank you for finding me friends in my time of need. Love Always.

Introduction

Her hands stilled, the knife frozen mid-slice. She forced herself to keep working, even as her heart began to race.

Jack entered through the side door, carrying a small cooler. His presence filled the room instantly, and Alexa felt a flush creeping up her neck. He looked relaxed in a faded T-shirt and cargo shorts, but there was a tension in his eyes that matched her own.

"Morning," he said casually, setting the cooler on the counter.

"Morning," Alexa replied, her voice strained. She kept her focus on the sandwiches, unwilling to meet his gaze.

Jack leaned against the counter, watching her. The silence between them was thick with unspoken words. Finally, he broke it.

"How's James?"

Alexa flinched at the question, her hands faltering. "He's fine," she said quickly. "Why?"

"No reason," Jack said, but his tone suggested otherwise. He paused, his voice softening. "You've been avoiding me."

Her breath caught. "I haven't."

"Yes, you have," Jack said, his voice steady but insistent. "And I get it. Last night was… complicated. But we can't just pretend it didn't happen."

Alexa's grip on the counter tightened. "We must, Jack. We don't have a choice."

He stepped closer, his voice dropping. "Don't we?"

The intensity of his gaze was almost too much to bear. Alexa felt the pull between them, the same magnetic force that had drawn them together the night before. But she couldn't let herself fall again.

"I can't do this," she whispered, shaking her head. "Not here. Not now."

Jack studied her for a moment, his expression unreadable. Then he stepped back, his jaw tightening. "Fine. But this isn't over, Alexa. You know it isn't.

CONTENTS PAGE

Chapter 1
The Morning After

Alexa Rivers woke to the sound of soft waves lapping against the dock, their rhythmic whispers carrying through the open window of the Lakehouse. The golden glow of the early morning sun spilled into the room, casting long, warm shadows across the cedar walls. She blinked, disoriented, her body heavy with exhaustion. The sheets were tangled around her legs, her skin damp with the remnants of last night's heat. For a moment, she felt the quiet peace that the Lakehouse always brought—a place where time seemed to slow, where the world outside felt like a distant dream.

And then it hit her.

The memory of Jack's touch, the way his hand lingered on her waist as they stood beneath the stars, the way his lips had brushed hers like a question she had been answering for years. Her stomach twisted as the events of the night flooded back in vivid detail.

Alexa sat up abruptly, her heart pounding. She pressed a hand to her mouth, as if trying to contain the emotions threatening to spill over. Upstairs, she could hear the faint creak of floorboards. James. Her husband of fifteen years. The man who had given her stability, a home, two beautiful children—and the man she had betrayed.

Her breath hitched as guilt crashed over her. She glanced toward the open window, where the lake stretched out in all its serene indifference. The Lakehouse had always been a sanctuary, a place for family gatherings and summer traditions. But now it felt like a witness, its wooden beams and familiar corners heavy with secrets.

Alexa swung her legs over the side of the bed, her feet brushing the cool wooden floor. She moved quietly, careful not to disturb James, though she knew he wouldn't be awake yet. He stayed up late last night with her brothers, drinking beers on the porch and reminiscing about old times.

Her movements were automatic as she pulled on a cardigan over her sleep shirt and stepped outside onto the wraparound deck. The crisp morning air hit her skin, making her shiver. The lake shimmered in the soft light, its surface calm and unbroken. But Alexa's mind was anything but still.

She leaned against the wooden railing, her hands gripping the weathered surface as she let her thoughts drift to Jack. Jack Hayes. Her best friend since childhood. The boy who had taught her how to ride a bike, who had held her hand when her parents fought, who had kissed her for the first time on the dock when they were sixteen.

How did we end up here?

The question haunted her as she remembered the way Jack had looked at her last night. His eyes, always warm and familiar, had burned with something deeper, something that had always been there but had finally broken free.

The memories came unbidden, pulling her back to the summers they'd spent at the Lakehouse. She could almost hear their laughter echoing across the water, feeling the sun on her skin as they drove off the dock together.

She thought of the summer when she turned sixteen, when everything between them had begun to shift. Jack had grown taller, his shoulders broader, his voice deeper. They had spent hours swimming in the lake, lying on the dock, and stealing moments away from the noise of their families.

One afternoon, they had taken the rowboat to the far side of the lake, where the trees grew thick, and the world felt untouchable. Alexa remembered how Jack had leaned back, his arms resting on the sides of the boat, and watched her with an intensity that made her heart race.

"You ever think about what it would be like if this was it?" he had asked, his voice low and quiet.

"If what was it?" she had replied, her cheeks flushing under his gaze.

"Just us. No one else. Just this."

She didn't know how to respond, her sixteen-year-old self both exhilarated and terrified by the weight of his words. Instead, she had splashed him with water, laughing nervously to break the tension. But the memory of his question had stayed with her, simmering quietly for years.

Alexa's mind snapped back to the present as the sound of the screen door creaking open behind her made her tense. She turned to see James stepping onto the deck, his hair rumpled from sleep, his face soft with the familiarity of a long marriage.

"Morning," he said, his voice still rough from the night before. He leaned against the doorway, his smile easy and unguarded.

"Morning," Alexa replied, forcing herself to return his smile.

James stepped toward her, wrapping an arm around her shoulders as he pressed a kiss to her temple. The gesture was automatic, comforting, but it didn't stir the same fire that Jack's touch had ignited.

She felt the guilt creep up her spine again, hot and unrelenting. She wanted to tell him to confess everything, but the words lodged in her throat. Instead, she leaned into his embrace, hoping he wouldn't notice the way her body stiffened.

"Are you okay?" he asked, his voice tinged with concern.

"I'm fine," she said quickly, pulling away. "Just tired."

-He nodded, accepting her answer without question. That was James—steady, dependable, and trusting. Alexa hated herself for the lies she was telling, not just to him but to herself.

As James returned inside to make coffee, Alexa's thoughts drifted once more to Jack. She could still feel the heat of his hand on her lower back, the way his breath had brushed against her ear when he leaned in close.

The evening had started innocently enough. The families had gathered around the firepit, roasting marshmallows and telling stories. Alexa had caught Jack watching her across the flames, his gaze intense but unreadable.

Later, as the others drifted off to bed, Jack had lingered. Alexa had stayed too, her heart pounding in her chest as the silence between them grew.

"You ever think about what it would've been like if things had been different?" he had asked, his voice low and rough.

Her heart had ached at the question, echoing the one he had asked all those years ago on the lake. She hadn't answered with words. Instead, she had stepped closer, her breath hitching as he reached for her.

The kiss had been slow at first, hesitant, as if they were both testing the limits of what they could allow themselves. But it had quickly deepened, years of longing and suppressed desire igniting into something neither of them could control.

Alexa looked out at the lake again, the surface now rippling gently in the breeze. The Lakehouse had always been a place of refuge, a place where she could escape the chaos of the outside world. But now it felt like a witness to her betrayal, its walls heavy with the memories of everything she had built and everything she had broken.

The house was filled with echoes of the past—her parents arguing in the kitchen, her brothers wrestling in the living room, her mother's laughter floating down the hall. And Jack. Always Jack.

She thought of the secret corners they had claimed as children, the dock where they had shared their first kiss, the trails they had explored together. The Lakehouse had seen it all, and now it carried the weight of a secret she wasn't sure she could bear.

As the morning sun climbed higher, Alexa felt the pull of two opposing forces, the fiery passion she had felt with Jack and the steady comfort of the life she had built with James.

Jack represented everything she had ever wanted but had been too afraid to reach for. He was freedom, adventure, and the embodiment of a love that felt like it could burn the world down.

James, on the other hand, was stability and safety. He was the man who had held her hand through the hardest moments of her life, who had given her two children and a home.

As much as she wanted to believe she could have both, Alexa knew that wasn't possible. She would have to make a choice, and no matter what she decided, someone would get hurt.

As the sounds of the Lakehouse stirred behind her—James humming in the kitchen, the kids laughing upstairs—Alexa took a deep breath, trying to steady herself.

For now, she would focus on the day ahead, on the family gathering that awaited them. But the question of what to do about Jack lingered in the back of her mind, a quiet storm threatening to break.

The lake stretched out before her, calm and unyielding, its surface hiding depths she wasn't sure she was ready to explore.

And as the sun rose higher, Alexa whispered to herself, "What have I done?"

Inside the Lakehouse, the smell of freshly brewed coffee wafted through the air. Alexa moved mechanically, her feet barely making a sound on the creaky floorboards. James stood at the kitchen counter, still in his faded pajama pants, pouring coffee into two mugs. He glanced at her as she stepped into the room, offering her the familiar, warm smile that used to make her feel safe.

"Figured you'd need this," he said, handing her a mug.

"Thanks," Alexa murmured, wrapping her hands around the ceramic cup. The warmth seeped into her palms, but it did little to ease the chill that had settled deep within her chest.

James took a seat at the small dining table, rubbing his hand over his face. "Last night was nice, wasn't it? Having everyone together again."

She nodded, her gaze fixed on the dark liquid in her cup. "Yeah. It was."

"Your brothers haven't changed much," he continued, chuckling. "Still trying to outdrink each other like we're in our twenties."

Alexa forced a small smile, her stomach tightening. She knew James was trying to fill the silence, oblivious to the turmoil brewing beneath her calm exterior. She hated herself for letting him carry on, for sitting there and pretending everything was fine.

The truth lingered on the tip of her tongue, heavy and suffocating. She glanced at James, at the faint lines around his eyes, the softness in his features that came from years of steady devotion. How could she destroy this? How could she shatter the life they had built together?

"Are you okay?" James asked, his voice cutting through her thoughts. His brow furrowed slightly as he studied her. "You seem… distracted."

"I'm fine," Alexa replied quickly, her voice too sharp. She softened it with a small smile. "Just tired. I didn't sleep well."

James nodded, seemingly satisfied with her answer, but his eyes lingered on her a moment longer before he returned to his coffee.

Alexa excused herself soon after, retreating to the solitude of the deck. The lake stretched out before her, its surface rippling gently in the breeze. She stood there, her hands gripping the wooden railing, her chest tightening with each passing second.

The memories of the night before refused to be silent.

She had told herself it was just the wine, the late hour, the nostalgia of being back at the Lakehouse. But deep down, she knew the truth. What had happened between her and Jack wasn't some fleeting mistake. It was years of longing, of suppressed emotions, bubbling to the surface in a moment that had felt inevitable.

Alexa closed her eyes, her mind replaying the scene like a film reel she couldn't stop. The way Jack had looked at her across the firepit, his eyes smoldering with unspoken words. The way her heart had raced when he'd lingered after everyone else had gone to bed. The way his touch had felt—electric, like coming home and setting herself ablaze all at once.

Her thoughts drifted further back to the day she had first met Jack. They were ten years old, and his family had just purchased the cabin next door. Alexa had been sitting on the dock, her legs dangling over the edge, when she heard a boy's laughter. She looked up to see Jack running along the shoreline, his blond hair shining in the sunlight, his smile wide and carefree.

"Hey!" he called out, waving as he approached. "What are you doing?"

"Fishing," Alexa replied, holding up the small rod in her hands.

He crouched down beside her, peering into the water. "Catch anything?"

"Not yet."

"Well, you're doing it wrong," he said confidently, He was carrying a fishing rod and they went fishing on his dad rowing boat.

Jack laughed, his eyes crinkling at the corners. "You'll catch more if you come to the other side of the lake. My dad says that's where the big ones are."

From that moment on, they were inseparable. Summers at the Lakehouse became their shared sanctuary, a place where the world felt smaller and simpler, where they could just be kids without the weight of expectations or responsibilities.

Over the years, their friendship deepened, shifting subtly as they grew older. Alexa remembered the summer when she turned sixteen, when she first began to see Jack in a new light. He had grown taller, his shoulders broader, his voice deeper. But it wasn't just his appearance that had changed, it was the way he looked at her, as if she were the center of his universe.

There had been a night that summer when they sat on the dock under a blanket of stars, the silence between them filled with possibilities. Jack had leaned back on his elbows, his gaze fixed on the sky.

"Do you ever think about the future?" he had asked.

“Sometimes,” Alexa replied. “What about you?”

He hesitated, then turned to look at her. “I think about us.”

Her heart had skipped a beat, but she had laughed it off, brushing it aside as teenage musing. She wasn’t ready to acknowledge the shift in their relationship, the way her heart raced whenever he was near. But the seed had been planted, and it continued to grow, quietly and steadily, over the years.

When Alexa met James in college, he had been everything she thought she wanted. He was steady, dependable, and kind—the perfect antidote to the unpredictability of her life. Her parents had divorced during her freshman year, and the Lakehouse had become a symbol of everything that was broken in her family.

James had been her anchor, helping her navigate the storm. He proposed after graduation, and they married the following year. Together, they built a life that was solid and predictable, a life that Alexa had convinced herself was enough.

But no matter how hard she tried, she couldn’t forget Jack. He remained a shadow in the corners of her mind, a quiet reminder of what could have been.

Alexa’s thoughts returned to the present, to the undeniable chemistry she had felt with Jack the night before.

It wasn't just the kiss, it was the way he had looked at her, the way his voice had softened when he said her name.

"Alexa," he had whispered, his breath warm against her skin. "I've waited for this. For you."

His words had pierced through her like a blade, cutting through the years of distance and doubt. In that moment, she had felt alive in a way she hadn't in years.

But now, in the harsh light of morning, the passion of the night before felt like a betrayal. She loved James—didn't she? He was her partner, the father of her children, the man who had stood by her through everything. But Jack was her heart, her soul, the part of herself she had buried long ago.

As the morning stretched on, Alexa knew she couldn't avoid Jack forever. He was still here, just next door, and the weight of their unspoken connection hung heavy in the air. She would have to face him, to confront the feelings she had tried so hard to suppress.

But for now, she would focus on the day ahead. There were family activities to plan, meals to prepare, and traditions to uphold. She would put on a brave face and pretend that everything was fine.

Yet deep down, she knew that nothing would ever be the same.

The lake stretched out before her, calm and unbroken, its surface, a mirror reflecting the storm within her. And as Alexa turned to go back inside, she whispered to herself, "What have I done?"

Alexa lingered on the deck long after James had retreated inside. The mug of coffee she clutched had gone cold, but she didn't notice. Her gaze remained fixed on the lake; it's still surface broken only by the occasional ripple from the breeze.

She replayed Jack's words from the night before in her mind: *"I've waited for this. For you."* The memory made her chest tighten, a mix of exhilaration and guilt that left her breathless.

The sound of laughter drifted through the open windows behind her, pulling her attention back to the present. The kids were awake now, their cheerful voices filling the house with life. Luke's boisterous energy clashed with Anna's quieter demeanor, but the two of them were inseparable when they were at the Lakehouse.

Alexa smiled faintly. This was why she had fought so hard to preserve the summer tradition. The Lakehouse wasn't just a place, it was a bridge connecting the past, present, and future. It was where she had found love, made mistakes, and built her life.

And yet, it was also the site of her greatest betrayal.

She heard the screen door creak open behind her and turned to see Luke bounding onto the deck, his hair messy and his face bright with excitement.

"Mom! Uncle Jake said he's taking us fishing! Can we go?"

Alexa forced a smile, masking the turmoil inside her. "Of course, sweetheart. Go grab your stuff, and I'll pack some snacks."

Luke beamed and dashed back inside, shouting something to Anna on his way. Alexa took a deep breath, bracing herself for the day ahead.

It was midmorning when Jack emerged from the guess room at the Lakehouse. Alexa was in the kitchen packing sandwiches for the fishing trip when she heard his voice outside—low, familiar, and unmistakable.

Her hands stilled, the knife frozen mid-slice. She forced herself to keep working, even as her heart began to race.

Jack entered through the side door, carrying a small cooler. His presence filled the room instantly, and Alexa felt a flush creeping up her neck. He looked relaxed in a faded T-shirt and cargo shorts, but there was a tension in his eyes that matched her own.

"Morning," he said casually, setting the cooler on the counter.

"Morning," Alexa replied, her voice strained. She kept her focus on the sandwiches, unwilling to meet his gaze.

Jack leaned against the counter, watching her. The silence between them was thick with unspoken words. Finally, he broke it.

"How's James?"

Alexa flinched at the question, her hands faltering. "He's fine," she said quickly. "Why?"

"No reason," Jack said, but his tone suggested otherwise. He paused, his voice softening. "You've been avoiding me."

Her breath caught. "I haven't."

"Yes, you have," Jack said, his voice steady but insistent. "And I get it. Last night was… complicated. But we can't just pretend it didn't happen."

Alexa's grip on the counter tightened. "We must, Jack. We don't have a choice."

He stepped closer, his voice dropping. "Don't we?"

The intensity of his gaze was almost too much to bear. Alexa felt the pull between them, the same magnetic force that had drawn them together the night before. But she couldn't let herself fall again.

"I can't do this," she whispered, shaking her head. "Not here. Not now."

Jack studied her for a moment, his expression unreadable. Then he stepped back, his jaw tightening. "Fine. But this isn't over, Alexa. You know it isn't.

With that, he grabbed the cooler and left, leaving Alexa standing in the kitchen, her emotions in turmoil.

The fishing trip provided a brief reprieve from the tension. Alexa joined James, her brothers, and the kids on the boat, trying to immerse herself in the simple joys of the moment. Luke was thrilled to catch his first fish, his excitement contagious.

James sat beside her; his arm draped casually over her shoulders. To anyone watching, they would have looked like the perfect family. But Alexa couldn't shake the heaviness in her chest.

"Are you okay?" James asked quietly, his voice laced with concern.

Alexa nodded, forcing a smile. "Just tired, that's all."

He seemed to accept her answer, but his eyes lingered on her for a moment longer, as if searching for something he couldn't quite find.

Later that afternoon, Alexa found herself alone in the attic, searching for an old board game at Luke's request. The attic was dimly lit, filled with the scent of cedar and dust. It was a time capsule of summer's past, with boxes of old photos, letters, and trinkets scattered across the space.

Her fingers brushed against a worn photo album, and she hesitated before opening it. The first picture she saw was of her and Jack, sitting side by side on the dock, their smiles wide and carefree. She was fifteen in the photo, her hair in messy braids, and Jack's arm was draped casually over her shoulders.

The sight of it brought a lump to her throat. Those summers had been the happiest of her life, but they had also laid the foundation for the ache she carried now.

Beneath the album was a stack of letters tied with a faded ribbon. Alexa recognized Bridgette's handwriting immediately. Her mother had always been meticulous about keeping correspondence, even in the days before email.

She untied the ribbon and began to read, her heart racing as she recognized the name in the first letter: *Michael.*

The letter was dated June 1986, written in Bridgette's elegant cursive.

My dearest Michael,

I can't stop thinking about you. Every time I'm at the Lakehouse, I feel your presence in the water, in the trees, in the air I breathe. It's as if you've become part of this place, part of me.

Alexa's breath hitched as she read the words. Her mother had always been a complicated figure—distant, demanding, and fiercely independent. But this letter revealed a vulnerability Alexa had never seen before.

She read through the stack, piecing together the story of an affair Bridgette had carried on for years. The letters were filled with passion and longing, but also with guilt. Bridgette had loved Michael deeply, but she had stayed with her husband for the sake of the family.

The parallels to her own situation were impossible to ignore. Alexa felt a pang of anger at Bridgette for keeping this secret, but also a deep sense of empathy.

Alexa sat on the attic floor; the letters spread out around her. The weight of her mother's choices—and the legacy of love and betrayal they carried—pressed down on her.

She thought of Jack, of the way his touch had ignited something inside her that she hadn't felt in years. She thought of James, of the life they had built together and the stability he provided.

And she thought of Bridgette, of the pain and sacrifice hidden behind her composed exterior.

For the first time, Alexa wondered if she was destined to repeat her mother's mistakes—or if she could find a way to break the cycle.

As the sun dipped below the horizon, casting the lake in hues of orange and gold, Alexa stood on the dock, her mind heavy with the weight of the day. The water was calm, its surface reflecting the fading light like a mirror.

She heard footsteps behind her and turned to see James approaching, his hands in his pockets. He joined her at the edge of the dock, his gaze fixed on the horizon.

"You've been quiet today," he said softly.

Alexa hesitated, her heart pounding. "Just a lot on my mind."

James nodded; his expression thoughtful. "This place does that to you, doesn't it? Makes you think about all the things you don't normally have time to."

Alexa swallowed hard, her throat tightening. She wanted to tell him everything—to confess her feelings for Jack, to share the letters she had found, to lay her heart bare. But the words wouldn't come.

Instead, she leaned into James, resting her head against his shoulder as they watched the sun disappear below the horizon. For now, she would hold onto the life she had, even as the pull of the past threatened to tear it apart.

Chapter 2
Summers of the Past

The Lakehouse always came alive in the summer. Its wooden beams soaked up the warmth of the sun, the creak of the screen door became a familiar rhythm, and the scent of pine and fresh water drifted in through every open window. For young Alexa Rivers, those summers at the Lakehouse felt like the kind of magic that could only exist in childhood—before the weight of the world settled onto your shoulders, before you began to understand what love and loss truly meant.

But even then, the magic was tinged with something heavier. Bridgette Rivers, Alexa's mother, had a way of ensuring that no joy was ever too pure, no moment too carefree. Her presence loomed over the Lakehouse like a shadow, her sharp voice and even sharper observations cutting through the lightness of the season.

This summer was no different. Alexa remembered when she met Jack Hayes who had moved into the cabin next door, and from the moment he arrived, her world began to shift.

Alexa had been sitting on the dock, her legs dangling over the edge, her toes grazing the cool water. She was fishing.

"Hey!" a voice called out, startling her.

She looked up to see a boy standing at the edge of the dock. He was about her age, ten, with sandy blond hair that stuck up in all directions and a wide, confident grin. He carried a fishing rod over his shoulder and a tackle box in his hand.

"Do you live here?" he asked.

"For the summer," Alexa replied, shielding her eyes from the sun to get a better look at him.

"Me too. I'm Jack." He dropped the tackle box and extended his hand, his grin widening.

"Alexa." She hesitated before shaking his hand, his palm warm and calloused against hers.

"You like fishing?" he asked, gesturing to the lake.

She wrinkled her nose. "Not really."

"Good," he said, laughing. "Because I'm terrible at it. You wanna come anyway?"

She hadn't planned to spend the afternoon with him, but something about his easy confidence and the way he seemed so at home in his skin made her say yes. They spent the rest of the day paddling around the lake in his family's rowboat,

Jack telling her stories about his school back home and how his older brother always beat him at basketball.

By the time the sun dipped below the horizon, painting the lake in hues of orange and gold, Alexa felt like she had known Jack her whole life.

From that day on, Alexa and Jack were inseparable. Every summer, they fell into a rhythm that felt as natural as breathing. They would wake up early to swim in the lake before breakfast, their laughter echoing across the water. In the afternoons, they explored the trails that wound through the forest, discovering hidden clearings and building forts out of fallen branches.

Jack taught her how to skip stones, his hand brushing against hers as he adjusted her grip. She never quite got the hang of it, but she loved the way his eyes lit up when she managed to make a stone hop across the water once or twice.

In the evenings, they would sit on the dock and watch the stars, their conversations growing deeper as they got older. Jack talked about wanting to be an architect, to design homes that felt as warm and welcoming as the Lakehouse. Alexa confessed her dream of becoming a writer, though she wasn't sure she had the talent.

"You'll be great," Jack said one night, his voice low and sure. "You've got that spark, Lex. I can see it."

She had blushed at the nickname, at the way his words made her feel like she was capable of anything.

But as close as Alexa and Jack became, their friendship didn't escape the notice of Bridgette Jones. Bridgette was a striking woman, with dark hair always swept into an elegant bun and eyes that seemed to pierce through whoever stood in front of her. She had a way of commanding attention, of making everyone around her feel small and uncertain.

"Jack Hayes," she said one afternoon, her tone sharp with disapproval. She was sitting on the porch, a glass of iced tea in one hand and a cigarette in the other, watching Alexa and Jack through the screen door. "The boy has no manners. Always shouting. Always running around barefoot."

Alexa bristled at her mother's words but said nothing. She had learned early on that it was better to let Bridgette's barbs pass without comment.

"He's a distraction," Bridgette continued, her gaze fixed on Alexa. "You're at an age where you should be focusing on your future, not wasting your time with a boy who doesn't have any ambition."

"He wants to be an architect," Alexa said quietly, her voice defensive despite herself.

Bridgette's lips curved into a thin smile. "We'll see."

It wasn't just Jack that Bridgette disapproved of—it was the very idea of Alexa forming a connection outside of the tightly controlled life Bridgette envisioned for her. Love, Bridgette had always said, was a weakness. It made people reckless. It made them vulnerable.

And yet, despite her mother's disapproval, Alexa couldn't stay away from Jack.

The summer Alexa turned sixteen was the summer everything changed. That year, the heat seemed to linger in the air, heavy and oppressive. The lake offered some relief, but even the water felt warmer than usual, as if the world itself was holding its breath.

One evening, a storm rolled in, the sky darkening with ominous clouds. Alexa and Jack were sitting on the dock, their legs dangling over the edge, when the first drops of rain began to fall.

"We should head back," Alexa said, glancing nervously at the sky.

"Not yet," Jack said, his voice soft. He was staring at the horizon, his expression thoughtful.

"What's wrong?" she asked.

He hesitated, then turned to look at her. "I need to tell you something."

Her heart skipped a beat at the intensity in his gaze. "What is it?"

He took a deep breath, his hands gripping the edge of the dock. "I… I think about you all the time, Lex. Not just here. All year long. I count down the days until summer, until I can see you again."

Alexa's chest tightened, her emotions swirling like the storm clouds above them. "Jack…"

"I know it's crazy," he said quickly, his words tumbling out. "But I can't help it. You're the only person who gets me. The only person who makes me feel like I'm enough."

The rain began to fall harder, the drops cold against Alexa's skin. She wanted to say something, to tell him that she felt the same way, but the weight of her mother's expectations held her back.

"I can't," she whispered, her voice barely audible over the sound of the rain. "Jack, I can't."

He looked at her, his face a mix of heartbreak and understanding. He nodded slowly, standing up and offering her his hand. "Come on," he said, his voice quiet. "Let's get inside."

That was the last summer Alexa and Jack spent together at the Lakehouse. The following year, Bridgette insisted that Alexa spend the summer interning for a family friend in

Boston, claiming it was a better use of her time. Jack wrote her letters, but she didn't reply. It was easier that way, easier to bury her feelings and focus on the path her mother had laid out for her.

But no matter how hard she tried, she couldn't forget the way Jack had looked at her that night on the dock, or the way his words had made her feel like she was standing on the edge of something terrifying and beautiful.

The days leading up to the summer storm had been filled with lightness, the kind of carefree joy that only seemed possible during those fleeting weeks at the Lakehouse. Alexa and Jack had spent their days swimming, fishing, and sneaking out late at night to sit on the dock under a canopy of stars.

Alexa could still remember the way Jack's laughter carried over the water, filling her chest with a warmth she didn't fully understand at the time. He had a way of making everything feel easier, lighter, as if the world wasn't as heavy as her mother always made it seem.

There was one afternoon that stood out in Alexa's mind. The sun had been blazing, and the lake had shimmered like glass. She and Jack had taken the rowboat out to the middle of the lake, where the water was the deepest and the air was filled with the scent of pine and wildflowers.

“You’re terrible at rowing,” Jack teased, grinning as Alexa struggled to keep the oars steady.

“I’m doing my best,” she shot back, her cheeks flushed from the effort.

“Here, let me.” He reached over to take the oars from her, his hands brushing against hers. The contact sent a jolt of electricity through her, though she tried to ignore it.

They sat in silence for a while as Jack rowed, the sound of the oars slicing through the water, the only noise. Alexa let her fingers trail in the cool water, watching the ripples spread out in delicate circles.

“Do you ever think about the future?” Jack asked suddenly, breaking the quiet.

Alexa looked up at him, startled by the question. “What do you mean?”

“I don’t know.” He shrugged, his eyes fixed on the horizon. “Like, where we’ll be in ten years. If we’ll still come here. If we’ll still be…” He trailed off, his voice soft.

Alexa’s chest tightened. She wanted to tell him that she couldn’t imagine a future without him, but the words felt too big, too heavy. Instead, she said, “I don’t know. I guess we’ll see.”

Jack looked at her then, his eyes searching hers as if trying to find an answer she wasn’t ready to give.

As much as Alexa cherished her time with Jack, those summers were always shadowed by her mother's presence. Bridgette had a way of making herself known, her sharp voice cutting through even the most peaceful moments.

One evening, Alexa had come inside after a long day with Jack to find Bridgette sitting at the kitchen table, a glass of wine in one hand and a cigarette in the other. The air was thick with smoke, the acrid smell clinging to the walls.

"You've been spending a lot of time with that boy," Bridgette said without looking up from her wineglass.

Alexa hesitated, her heart sinking. "He's, my friend."

"Friend," Bridgette repeated, her tone laced with skepticism. She finally looked up, her piercing gaze making Alexa squirm. "You're getting too close, Alexa. Boys like that—boys with no direction, no ambition—they'll only hold you back."

"That's not true," Alexa said, her voice shaking. "He's smart. He wants to be an architect."

Bridgette's laugh was sharp, almost cruel. "Dreams don't pay the bills, darling. And they certainly don't build a future."

Alexa clenched her fists, anger and frustration bubbling inside her. "You don't know him."

"I know enough," Bridgette said, her voice cold. "You're better than this, Alexa. You have potential. Don't waste it on someone who can't give you what you deserve."

Alexa wanted to argue, to defend Jack, but the words caught in her throat. She felt small and powerless under her mother's scrutiny, just as she always did.

The storm had been building all day, the sky growing darker and the air heavier with each passing hour. By evening, the Lakehouse was bathed in an eerie light, the wind howling through the trees.

Alexa and Jack had spent the afternoon on the dock, watching the storm roll in. The air was charged, and not just because of the weather. There was an unspoken tension between them, a sense that something was shifting.

When the first drops of rain began to fall, Jack turned to her, his expression serious. "Come on," he said, holding out his hand. "Let's go inside."

Alexa hesitated, her heart racing. "Wait," she said, her voice barely audible over the sound of the wind.

"What is it?" Jack asked, his brow furrowing.

She opened her mouth to speak, but the words wouldn't come. Instead, she shook her head and stood, brushing past him as she made her way toward the house.

Jack followed; his footsteps heavy behind her. By the time they reached the porch, the rain was coming down in sheets, soaking them both to the bone.

"Alexa," Jack said, his voice sharp.

She turned to face him, her chest heaving. "What?"

He stepped closer, his eyes blazing. "Why are you pulling away?

"I'm not," she said, though the lie tasted bitter.

"Yes, you are," he insisted. "You've been doing it all summer. Every time I try to get close, you shut me out. Why?"

Alexa's throat tightened, tears pricking her eyes. "Because I can't, Jack. I can't be what you want me to be."

"And what do I want you to be?" he asked, his voice softer now.

She hesitated, her heart breaking as she looked at him. "Everything."

Jack stared at her for a long moment, the rain dripping from his hair and running down his face. Finally, he nodded, his jaw tightening. "Okay," he said, his voice barely above a whisper.

He turned and walked away, leaving Alexa standing on the porch, the storm raging around her.

The next morning, the storm passed, leaving the lake calm and still. But something between Alexa and Jack had shifted, something that couldn't be undone.

They spent the rest of the summer in a strained silence, their easy laughter and stolen moments replaced by awkward exchanges and quiet tension. When it was time for Alexa to leave, they said their goodbyes on the dock, their words heavy with everything they didn't say.

"Good luck," Jack said, his voice flat.

"You too," Alexa replied, her heart aching.

As the boat pulled away, Alexa looked back at Jack, standing alone on the dock. She wanted to call out to him; to tell him how much he meant to her, but the words stayed trapped in her chest.

Years later, as Alexa stood on the same dock, watching the sunrise, she couldn't help but think of that summer. The storm, the laughter, the heartbreak all felt so vivid, as if no time had passed at all.

She wondered if Jack still thought about her, if he remembered the way they used to be. And she wondered if things could have been different, if she had been brave enough to follow her heart instead of her mother's expectations.

But the past was the past, and no amount of wishing could change it.

As the sun rose higher, painting the lake in hues of gold and pink, Alexa took a deep breath and let the memories wash over her. They were bittersweet, but they were hers.

And for now, that was enough.

The last few days before Alexa's sixteenth summer came to an end were defined by avoidance. After the storm and Jack's unspoken confession, they had fallen into a strained silence that seemed capable of breaking. Alexa could feel Jack's presence in every corner of the Lakehouse, and yet he was suddenly unreachable.

Every morning, she saw him by the dock, skipping stones or reading a book, but she didn't join him. Every evening, as the sun sank below the trees, she heard his footsteps on the trails that wove through the woods, but she stayed on the porch, nursing her mother's bitter comments about how she should have been preparing for a "better life."

She wanted to tell him something, anything, but she was too afraid of what it would mean. Bridgette's disapproving words echoed in her mind: *"Boys like Jack will ruin you."*

On the second-to-last day, Alexa decided to write him a letter. She sat cross-legged on her bed, a notebook open in her lap, as she tried to put her feelings into words.

Dear Jack,

I don't know how to say this out loud, but I'm sorry. I'm sorry for pulling away, for not being brave enough to tell you how much you mean to me. You're my best friend. You always have been. And I think—no, I know—that what I feel for you is more than friendship.

The pen trembled in her hand as she stared at the words. Could she give this to him? Could she tell him everything before she left?

She folded the page and tucked it into an envelope, sealing it with a trembling breath. But when she saw him sitting on the dock later that afternoon, the letter remained in her pocket. She couldn't bring herself to give it to him.

That night, Alexa sat on the dock alone, the envelope still in her pocket. The water was calm, and the stars reflected on its surface like scattered diamonds. She clutched the letter tightly, wondering if she would ever have the courage to say what needed to be said.

The final evening of the summer was marked by a tension Alexa couldn't escape. Bridgette had summoned her to the kitchen, her voice sharp with authority.

"You leave tomorrow," Bridgette said, pouring herself a glass of wine. "I hope you've spent this summer wisely."

Alexa frowned, unsure of what her mother meant. "I've done everything you asked, haven't I? I've been studying and helping with the house—"

"That's not what I mean." Bridgette's eyes narrowed as she turned to face Alexa. "You've spent too much time with that boy."

"Jack isn't—" Alexa began, but Bridgette cut her off.

"Don't argue with me. I've seen the way you look at him, the way he looks at you. You're too young to understand what you're doing, Alexa, but I do." Bridgette's voice softened, but her words were no less cutting. "I've lived through what happens when you let your heart lead you astray. It ruins you. It makes you weak."

Alexa swallowed the lump in her throat. "I don't—"

"You're leaving tomorrow," Bridgette said, her tone final. "And I don't want to hear another word about Jack Hayes. Do you understand me?"

Alexa nodded, her chest tight with a mix of anger and sadness. She didn't trust herself to speak.

As Alexa sat on the dock now, all those years later, she couldn't help but think of that moment. She had kept the letter all this time, tucked away in a box of memories she couldn't bear to part with.

She pulled it out now, unfolding the yellowed paper with trembling hands. The words she had written so long ago stared back at her, a reminder of the love she had never been brave enough to claim.

She wondered if Jack still thought about her, if he remembered the summers they had shared at the Lakehouse. Did he regret the way things ended? Did he still feel the same pull she felt every time she thought of him?

The sound of the lake lapping against the dock brought her back to the present. She folded the letter and tucked it back into her pocket, her heart heavy with the weight of the past.

As the sun began to set, casting the lake in hues of gold and orange, Alexa whispered to herself, “I’m sorry, Jack.”

And for the first time in years, she let herself cry.

She analyzed that day again. The morning of Alexa’s departure felt eerily still. The lake, usually alive with movement and birdsong, mirrored the somber atmosphere that hung over the house. Bridgette moved through the kitchen with purpose, her heels clicking on the hardwood floor as she finalized their travel arrangements.

“Don’t dawdle,” she called over her shoulder to Alexa, who stood by the doorway, her suitcase already packed. “We need to be on the road before lunch.”

Alexa barely acknowledged her mother's command, her eyes drifting toward the dock. She hoped Jack would appear, even if just to say goodbye. But the dock remained empty, the lake stretching out into the distance like a reflection of her own uncertainty.

Bridgette noticed her lingering gaze and narrowed her eyes. "Stop waiting for him. You've already said your goodbyes."

"I wasn't waiting," Alexa lied, her voice hollow.

Bridgette's lips pressed into a thin line, her expression unreadable. "Good," she said curtly, turning back to her coffee.

With only an hour left before they left, Alexa found herself drawn to the dock one last time. She walked slowly, her steps heavy with reluctance. Each creak of the wooden boards beneath her feet felt like a farewell, the memories of countless summers flooding back with every step.

She sat down, dangling her legs over the edge, just as she and Jack had done so many times before. The gentle lapping of the water against the posts was the only sound, a quiet rhythm that seemed to echo the ache in her chest.

Alexa reached into her pocket and pulled out the letter she had written to Jack. The envelope was slightly crumpled from being carried around, its edges worn from the countless times she had considered handing it to him.

She unfolded the letter and read it again, the words feeling both foreign and deeply familiar:

Dear Jack,
I'm sorry for pulling away. I'm sorry for not being braver, for not saying the things I should have said. You're my best friend, but you're also so much more than that. I don't know what the future looks like, but I know it feels empty without you in it.

Her hands trembled as she folded the letter again, tears blurring her vision. She thought about leaving it for him, tucking it somewhere he might find it later. But the thought of him reading it, of him knowing how she truly felt, made her chest tighten with fear.

"Alexa."

The sound of Jack's voice startled her, and she quickly wiped at her cheeks, shoving the letter back into her pocket. She turned to see him standing at the edge of the dock, his hands in his pockets, his expression guarded.

"You're here," she said softly, her voice barely above a whisper.

"I wasn't going to let you leave without saying goodbye," he replied, stepping closer.

She stood, her heart pounding as he stopped a few feet away from her. For a moment, neither of them spoke. The air between them felt charged, like the calm before a storm.

"I wanted to see you," Alexa admitted, her voice trembling.

"I know," Jack said, his gaze fixed on her. "I did too."

The weight of their unspoken feelings hung between them, heavy and suffocating. Alexa wanted to say something, to tell him everything that was in her heart, but the words wouldn't come.

"Do you have to go?" Jack asked, his voice quiet but filled with longing.

She nodded, her throat tightening. "I do."

His jaw clenched, and he looked away, his hands balling into fists at his sides. "I wish things were different."

"Me too," she whispered.

He took a deep breath, his shoulders slumping as he turned back to her. "Take care of yourself, okay?"

"You too," Alexa said, tears spilling over her cheeks.

For a moment, she thought he might say more, but instead, he stepped forward and pulled her into a hug. His arms wrapped around her tightly, and she buried her face against his shoulder, wishing she could freeze the moment and stay there forever.

When they finally pulled apart, Jack gave her a small, sad smile. "Goodbye, Lex." "Goodbye, Jack," she whispered, her voice breaking.

He turned and walked away, his footsteps fading as he disappeared down the path. Alexa watched him go, her heart aching with every step he took.

The drive back to Boston was quiet. Bridgette focused on the road, her sharp features unreadable as she navigated the winding highways. Alexa stared out the window, the landscape blurring past her, though she hardly noticed. Her mind was still at the Lakehouse, on the dock, with Jack.

"Stop sulking," Bridgette said after a while, her tone clipped. "You'll thank me someday."

"For what?" Alexa asked, her voice flat.

"For keeping you focused," Bridgette replied. "That boy would have distracted you, and you'd have wasted your potential. You'll see, Alexa. You'll understand when you're older."

Alexa didn't respond. She turned her gaze back to the window, biting her lip to keep from saying the things she knew would only lead to another argument.

Now, sitting on the dock all those years later, Alexa thought about how much her mother's words had shaped her life. At the time, she had believed Bridgette was right—that letting Jack go was the only way to protect her future.

But what about the cost?

She reached into her pocket and pulled out the letter she had never given to Jack. The paper was worn, the ink slightly faded, but the words still held all the weight they had when she first wrote them.

She unfolded it slowly, her hands trembling as she read it again. "I should have given it to you," she whispered to the empty air, her voice trembling. "I should have been brave enough to fight for us."

The water lapped gently against the dock, as if offering comfort. Alexa closed her eyes, letting the memories of Jack's touch, his laugh, his voice wash over her.

She didn't know if he still thought of her, if he still carried the same ache she did. But as the sun set over the lake, painting the world in hues of gold and orange, she made a silent promise to herself: she wouldn't let fear hold her back anymore.

Chapter 3

Marriage and Motherhood

The late morning sun spilled through the kitchen windows of the Lakehouse, casting a golden light on James as he flipped pancakes on the griddle. Alexa stood by the counter, slicing strawberries for breakfast, her hands moving with practiced ease. The smell of coffee mingled with the faint scent of pine that drifted in from the open window. It was a scene that could have been pulled from any of their summers here—safe, routine, ordinary.

She watched James as he worked, his brow furrowed in concentration. He hummed softly to himself, a tune she didn't recognize. It was one of the many little things she had once loved about him, his quiet ability to fill a space without demanding attention. But now, as she stood there, she felt a pang of guilt. She wondered when exactly it had started—this distance between them, the unspoken gap that seemed to widen with each passing year.

Alexa's mind drifted, unbidden, to Jack. The memory of his hand on hers, the way his voice had softened when he said her name, it felt as vivid now as it had that night by the lake. She shook her head, trying to banish the thought.

James turned to her, offering her a plate of pancakes. "Do you think we should head into town later? Luke was asking about that old ice cream shop."

Alexa forced a smile. "Sure. That sounds nice."

James's expression softened, his eyes crinkling at the corners. "You, okay? You've seemed… distracted this week."

"I'm fine," Alexa replied quickly, her voice betraying her.

He studied her for a moment, but before he could press further, Luke and Anna came barreling into the kitchen, their laughter breaking the tension.

As Alexa watched James interact with the kids, she felt a familiar ache, a mix of gratitude and guilt. James had been her anchor, the one who had steadied her when her life had felt like it was unraveling.

She thought back to the day they met in college, during her sophomore year. It had been just a few months after her mother's death, and Alexa had been drowning in grief. She had thrown herself into her classes, using academics to escape the suffocating sadness that seemed to follow her everywhere.

One afternoon, she had been sitting in the campus library, staring blankly at her notebook, when James had approached her.

"Mind if I sit here?" he had asked, gesturing to the empty chair across from her.

She had nodded without looking up, assuming he would keep to himself. But instead, he had struck up a conversation, asking her about her classes, her interests, her plans for the future.

There had been something calming about his presence, a quiet steadiness that made her feel safe in a way she hadn't felt in months. They began meeting in the library regularly, and before long, their study sessions turned into coffee dates, then dinners, then late-night talks about their hopes and dreams.

James had been the first-person Alexa had opened to about her mother. She still remembered the way he had held her hand as she cried, his thumb brushing soothingly over her knuckles.

"She'd be proud of you," he had said softly. "You're stronger than you think."

In that moment, Alexa had realized that James was exactly what she needed—someone who would be there for her, who would never let her fall.

Their early years together had been filled with promises. They had graduated, moved to the city, and built a life that felt stable and secure. James got a job at a marketing firm, while Alexa pursued freelance writing. They spent their weekends exploring the city, trying new restaurants, and dreaming about the future.

When James proposed, it wasn't a grand, dramatic gesture. It was quiet and intimate, just the two of them sitting on a park bench.

"I don't want to do this life without you," he had said simply, holding out a small velvet box.

Alexa had said yes without hesitation, feeling a sense of certainty she hadn't felt since she was a child.

The memory of their wedding day was tinged with bittersweet emotions. It had been a beautiful ceremony, held in a small garden surrounded by their closest friends and family. Alexa had worn a simple lace dress, her hair loose around her shoulders, and James had looked at her like she was the only person in the world.

But even then, there had been a small, quiet voice in the back of her mind. She had pushed it away, telling herself that she was choosing the right path, the safe path.

As they danced under the twinkling lights of the reception, Alexa had caught a glimpse of her reflection in the glass of the venue's doors. For a moment, she thought she saw Jack standing there, watching her. She had blinked, and the image was gone, but the ghost of it stayed with her.

Over the years, Alexa and James had built a life that looked perfect on the outside. They had moved to the suburbs, bought a charming house, and had two beautiful children, Anna and Luke.

Alexa adored being a mother. She loved the way Anna's eyes lit up when she talked about her latest science project, the way Luke's laughter filled the house when he told one of his goofy jokes. She cherished the quiet moments, like reading bedtime stories or baking cookies on rainy afternoons.

But as much as she loved her children, she couldn't shake the feeling that she was losing herself. Her days were filled with soccer practices, parent-teacher conferences, and grocery runs. She had traced her dreams of being a writer for the reality of being a wife and mother, and while she didn't regret it, there was a part of her that longed for something more.

The Lakehouse was supposed to be a place of rest, a break from the monotony of everyday life. But this summer, it felt like a reminder of everything Alexa had left behind.

She watched James as he played cards with the kids on the porch, his laughter blending with theirs. He looked so at ease, so content, and Alexa felt a pang of guilt.

This was the life they had built together—the life they had chosen. And yet, her mind kept drifting to Jack.

She thought about the way his eyes had lingered on hers during their last conversation, the way his presence seemed to fill every corner of the Lakehouse.

Alexa struggled with the duality of her emotions. She loved James in a quiet, steady way, the way you love someone who has shared your life for so many years. But with Jack, it was different. It was fire and longing, a passion that burned even brighter because it had been denied for so long.

When James reached for her hand, it felt familiar, like a well-worn routine. But when Jack's hand had brushed hers, it had sent a jolt of electricity through her that she couldn't ignore.

The guilt was overwhelming. How could she feel this way about Jack when James had given her so much? When he had stood by her through every challenge, every heartbreak?

As the sun set over the lake, casting the water in hues of gold and pink, Alexa sat on the porch, watching her family. James was helping Luke set up a telescope, his patient voice as he explained how to adjust the focus.

It was a picture-perfect moment, the kind of scene she had always imagined when she thought about her future.

But as much as she tried to convince herself that this was enough, she couldn't shake the feeling that something was missing.

Marriage, she realized, wasn't just about love. It was about compromise, sacrifice, and choosing each other every day—even when it wasn't easy.

And yet, as much as she wanted to choose James, there was a part of her that couldn't let go of Jack.

The summer breeze rustled through the porch as James adjusted the telescope for Luke, his calm voice explaining each step. Alexa stayed seated in the rocking chair; her gaze fixed on her husband. He had always been patient, the kind of man who never rushed through life's moments. He was the rock their family leaned on, a source of steady, unwavering love.

When they first started dating in college, that steadiness had been exactly what Alexa needed. She was still reeling from her mother's death, lost in a sea of grief, when James had come into her life like a lifeboat. He didn't try to fix her; he just stayed by her side, his quiet strength pulling her out of the darkness.

She remembered one particularly hard night when she had broken down in his dorm room. She'd cried for hours, pouring out all the hurt she had buried inside. James hadn't said much—he rarely did in moments like that—but he held her, his arms a haven in a world that felt chaotic and cruel.

"You don't have to be strong all the time," he'd said softly, his fingers brushing through her hair. "It's okay to let someone else carry the weight for a while."

That was James. The man who had taught her that love didn't have to be fiery or intense to be real. It could be quiet, gentle, and enduring.

But over the years, their relationship had shifted. The spark that had once drawn them together had faded, replaced by the routines of everyday life. James's touch, once so comforting, now felt predictable. Their conversations had grown shallow, revolving around schedules, bills, and the kids' activities.

Alexa hated admitting it—even to herself—but there were times she felt like they were more roommates than partners.

The last time James had kissed her with real passion was months ago, during their anniversary dinner. He had leaned across the table, his smile warm and inviting, and kissed her the way he used to when they first started dating. For a moment, Alexa had felt a flicker of the old spark, but it had faded as quickly as it came.

Now, sitting on the porch, she watched him laugh with Luke, his voice carrying over the gentle sounds of the lake. She loved him—of course she did. But that love felt like a quiet hum compared to the roaring fire she had felt when Jack's hand brushed hers just days ago.

As the evening wore on, Alexa found herself in the kitchen, preparing dinner while the kids played outside. She could hear Anna and Luke arguing over whose turn it was to use the telescope, their voices filled with the kind of carefree joy that only came with childhood.

Alexa's chest tightened. She loved her children more than anything, but lately, she had felt like she was failing them. She was always there physically—packing their lunches, driving them to soccer games, helping with homework—but she worried that she wasn't fully present.

Anna, at sixteen, was growing more distant. She spent most of her time in her room or on her phone, emerging only when necessary. Alexa tried to connect with her, but every attempt was met with an eye roll or a curt response.

And Luke, at eleven, was still eager for her attention, but Alexa feared it wouldn't last. She knew the teenage years would pull him away, just as they had with Anna.

She thought about how her own mother had been during her teenage years—aloof, critical, and distant. Alexa had vowed she would never be like Bridgette, but there were times she caught herself snapping at Anna in a way that felt too familiar.

"Mom!" Luke's voice cut through her thoughts, and she turned to see him standing in the doorway, his face flushed with excitement. "Come outside! The stars are amazing!"

Alexa smiled, wiping her hands on a towel. "I'll be there in a minute."

Luke ran off, and Alexa took a deep breath. She needed to be present for them, to push away the guilt and the thoughts of Jack and focus on the life she had built.

Later that night, as Alexa lay in bed beside James, her mind drifted to their wedding day. It had been a perfect spring afternoon, the garden filled with blooming flowers and the soft hum of laughter.

James had looked at her with so much love in his eyes as she walked down the aisle. For a moment, she had felt like the luckiest woman in the world.

But there was a moment, just before the ceremony, when doubt had crept in. As she stood in front of the mirror, adjusting her veil, she had thought about Jack. She hadn't seen him in years, but his memory had lingered, a quiet presence in the back of her mind.

Her best friend, Rachel, had noticed her hesitation. "You okay?" she'd asked, her brow furrowed with concern.

"I'm fine," Alexa had lied, forcing a smile.

But as James took her hands during their vows, her doubts had melted away. In that moment, she had believed with all her heart that she was making the right choice.

Now, lying beside him, she wondered if she had been wrong.

The Lakehouse was filled with Jack's presence. Every creak of the floorboards, every rustle of the trees outside, seemed to remind her of him. She couldn't stop thinking about the way his voice had sounded when he said her name, the way his touch had sent shivers down her spine.

She felt guilty for thinking about him, for letting her mind wander to the what-ifs when James was lying right beside her. But she couldn't help it. Jack had always been the question she never dared to answer, the road she hadn't taken.

She thought about their teenage summers, the way he had made her laugh until her stomach hurt, the way his eyes had always seemed to find hers in a crowded room. She thought about the storm, the night he had almost told her everything, and the way she had walked away.

And she thought about the kiss they had shared just days ago, the culmination of years of longing and unspoken feelings.

Alexa rolled over, staring at the ceiling. Marriage, she realized, was never as simple as the fairy tales made it seem. It wasn't just about love, it was about compromise, sacrifice, and choosing each other every day, even when it was hard.

She loved James. She did. But she couldn't deny that something was missing, that the life they had built together, as perfect as it seemed on the outside, didn't quite fill the void in her heart.

She wanted to believe that they could find their way back to each other, that the spark they had once shared could be reignited. But she also couldn't ignore the pull she felt toward Jack, the part of her that had never truly let him go.

As the sound of James's steady breathing filled the room, Alexa closed her eyes, her mind a whirlwind of memories, regrets, and questions.

Could she choose passion over stability? Fire over comfort? Could she risk everything she had built for the chance to feel alive again?

The answers eluded her, but one thing was clear, something had to change.

The next morning, Alexa woke before anyone else. The Lakehouse was bathed in the soft glow of dawn, the world outside still wrapped in a peaceful hush. She slipped out of bed, careful not to wake James, and made her way to the kitchen.

Pouring herself a cup of coffee, she moved to the porch, where the lake stretched out before her like a mirror reflecting the sky. It was moments like these—when the world seemed to stand still—that she felt the full weight of her choices pressing down on her.

The steam rose from her mug, curling into the crisp morning air. She thought about James, still asleep upstairs. He had always been there for her, steady and reliable, the kind of partner she had once believed she needed. But their life together had settled into a predictable routine, one that left her feeling both safe and stifled.

Her mind wandered, unbidden, to Jack. His name alone sent a thrill through her, a reminder of the passion and possibility she had buried long ago. She hated herself for thinking of him, for allowing his presence to intrude on these quiet moments. But the truth was, she couldn't stop.

A movement in her peripheral vision caught her attention, and she turned to see Anna emerging from the house, her long hair tied back in a messy ponytail. Her daughter rarely rose early, but today she seemed different—restless, maybe even troubled.

"Morning, Mom," Anna said, her voice quiet as she joined Alexa on the porch.

"Morning, sweetheart," Alexa replied, gesturing to the empty chair beside her. "What's got you up so early?"

Anna shrugged, pulling her knees to her chest as she stared out at the lake. "Couldn't sleep, I guess."

Alexa sipped her coffee, waiting for Anna to say more. She had learned that her daughter rarely opened when prompted; it was better to let her come to it in her own time.

"Do you ever feel like you don't know what you're supposed to be doing?" Anna asked suddenly, her voice tentative.

Alexa blinked, surprised by the question. "What do you mean?"

Anna sighed, resting her chin on her knees. "I don't know. I just… I feel like everyone expects me to have it all figured out, but I don't. I don't even know what I want."

Alexa's heart ached at the vulnerability in her daughter's voice. She reached over, placing a hand on Anna's arm. "It's okay not to know, Anna. You're sixteen. You don't have to have everything figured out right now."

"But you and Dad did," Anna said, glancing at her. "You knew what you wanted, didn't you?"

Alexa hesitated, her chest tightening. "Not always," she admitted softly. "There were times I wasn't sure. Times I had to figure it out as I went."

Anna nodded; her expression thoughtful. "Did you ever regret any of it?"

The question hung in the air, heavy with unspoken meaning. Alexa's mind flashed to Jack, to the life she might have had if she had made different choices.

"I think everyone has regrets," she said carefully. "But I try not to let them define me. What matters is what you do with the choices you make."

Anna didn't respond, but Alexa could see the wheels turning in her daughter's mind.

Later that morning, Alexa found herself in the kitchen with James. He was chopping vegetables for lunch; his movements deliberate and precise. It was a small thing, but it reminded her of why she had fallen for him in the first place, his quiet attention to detail, his ability to bring order to chaos.

"You seemed deep in thought earlier," James said, glancing at her. "Everything okay?"

Alexa hesitated, unsure how to answer. "Just thinking about the kids," she said finally.

James nodded, his expression softening. "Anna's been a little off lately, hasn't she? I worry about her."

"She'll be okay," Alexa said, though she wasn't sure if she was trying to convince James or herself.

James set down the knife and turned to face her, his gaze steady. "And what about you?"

"What about me?"

"You've been distant," he said, his voice gentle but firm. "Not just here, but for a while now. I feel like you're carrying something, but you won't let me in."

Alexa's chest tightened. She wanted to tell him to spill everything she was feeling, but the words wouldn't come. How could she explain the storm of emotions swirling inside her without breaking him?

"I'm just tired," she said, forcing a smile. "That's all."

James didn't look convinced, but he let it go. "Maybe we should take a day, just the two of us," he suggested. "Go into town, have lunch somewhere nice. What do you think?"

Alexa nodded, though the thought of spending the day alone with James filled her with a mix of longing and dread. "I'd like that."

That afternoon, Alexa found herself alone on the porch again, her journal open in her lap. Writing had always been her escape, her way of making sense of the chaos in her mind. But today, the words wouldn't come.

She stared at the blank page, her pen hovering above it. The memories of her time with Jack, the choices she had made, and the life she had built with James all swirled together, leaving her feeling unmoored.

She thought back to her wedding day, to the vows she had spoken with trembling hands. She had meant every word at the time, but now, she wasn't sure if she could live up to them.

She thought about her children, about the example she set for them. Would they look back on her life and see a woman who had settled for stability, or a woman who had fought for what she truly wanted?

The sound of footsteps on the porch pulled her from her thoughts. She looked up to see Anna standing there, her expression uncertain.

"Mom, can we talk?"

"Of course," Alexa said, closing her journal and gesturing for Anna to sit beside her.

Anna hesitated, then sat down, her hands twisting nervously in her lap. "I've been thinking about what you said earlier," she began. "About choices and regrets."

Alexa nodded, waiting for her to continue.

"I think I'm scared of making the wrong choice," Anna admitted. "Like, what if I pick something and it ruins everything?"

Alexa reached over, taking her daughter's hands in hers. "Sweetheart, there's no such thing as a perfect choice. Every decision you make will have its ups and downs, its challenges and rewards. The important thing is to trust yourself and know that you're strong enough to handle whatever comes next.

Anna looked at her, her eyes searching for Alexa's face. "Did you always trust yourself?"

Alexa hesitated, her mind flashing to Jack and the choices she had made. "Not always," she said honestly. "But I've learned that even when you doubt yourself, you can still find a way forward."

Anna nodded, a small smile tugging at the corners of her lips. "Thanks, Mom."

That night, as Alexa lay in bed beside James, her mind once again drifted to Jack. She couldn't stop herself from wondering what he was doing, where he was, if he was thinking about her too.

She knew it was wrong to dwell on him, to let his memory intrude on her life with James. But no matter how hard she tried, she couldn't let him go.

The Lakehouse seemed to hold his presence, his laughter echoing in the corners of her mind. It was as if he were a part of the very foundation of the house, a constant reminder of the road she hadn't taken.

As she stared at the ceiling, her heart heavy with guilt and longing, Alexa whispered into the darkness, "What do I do now?"

The answer, if there was one, didn't come.

The Lakehouse was silent that night, save for the faint rustling of leaves outside the window. Alexa lay in bed, staring at the ceiling as James's even breathing filled the room. She had spent the entire day trying to focus on her family—on Luke's excited chatter about his telescope, on

Anna's guarded attempts to open, and on James's gentle insistence that they take a moment for themselves. Yet, even now, in the stillness of the evening, her thoughts betrayed her.

She turned her head to look at James. His features were soft in sleep, his brow smooth and his mouth slightly open. He looked peaceful, unburdened. Alexa envied him for that. She envied his ability to exist in the world they had built together without questioning its foundation.

She shifted slightly, careful not to disturb him. Her thoughts drifted to Jack, as they so often did when the house was quiet. She could still feel the warmth of his touch, the intensity of his gaze. It wasn't just the memory of him that haunted her—it was the possibility of what they could have been.

Alexa closed her eyes, willing herself to let it go, to focus on the life she had chosen. But the truth was, she felt caught between two worlds, the safe, steady life she had built with James and the fiery, untamed love she had always felt for Jack.

Earlier that evening, after dinner, Alexa had found Anna sitting on the dock, her legs dangling over the edge. The girl's usual air of detachment was replaced by something softer, more reflective. Alexa had joined her, sitting close but not too close, giving her space to speak if she wanted to.

"Do you ever feel like you don't know who you are anymore?" Anna asked suddenly, her voice quiet but steady.

Alexa's heart ached at the vulnerability in her daughter's words. She had felt the same way so many times—lost in the roles she played as a wife, a mother, a daughter.

"Sometimes," Alexa admitted. "I think it's normal to feel that way, especially when you're trying to figure out where you fit in the world."

Anna nodded, her gaze fixed on the rippling water. "I just feel like everyone expects me to be someone I'm not."

Alexa wanted to tell her that she understood that she had spent her entire life trying to meet other people's expectations. Instead, she placed a hand on Anna's shoulder, offering silent reassurance.

"You don't have to have it all figured out right now," Alexa said softly. "Just focus on what makes you happy, and the rest will come."

Anna turned to her, her expression thoughtful. "Thanks, Mom."

Now, lying in bed, Alexa replayed the conversation in her mind. She wondered if she had taken her own advice, if she had ever truly focused on what made her happy. Or had she spent her entire life chasing stability at the expense of passion?

The Lakehouse held so many memories, so many moments of joy and heartbreak. It was a place where she had found love, lost it, and built a life that looked perfect on the surface. But beneath that surface, she was drowning in doubt.

As the moonlight filtered through the curtains, Alexa whispered into the darkness, “What do I do?”

The only response was the sound of the lake, its gentle waves lapping against the shore.

Chapter 4
The Weight of Secrets

The Lakehouse seemed smaller with Jack there, as though his presence filled the space in a way no one else ever could. Alexa felt it in the charged air between them, in the way her heart raced whenever their paths crossed. It wasn't just his presence; it was the weight of their shared history, the echoes of the years that had come before this moment.

That morning, Alexa had escaped to the garden, hoping the fresh air would clear her mind. The kids were out by the dock with James, their laughter carrying across the still lake. She could hear Luke shouting instructions to Anna about fishing, James's deep voice chiming in occasionally. It should have been a peaceful scene, the kind of moment she usually cherished. But Alexa couldn't focus.

"Thought I might find you here," Jack's voice broke through her thoughts.

She turned sharply, her breath catching as she saw him standing a few feet away, his hands shoved into his pockets. He was wearing a faded button-down shirt and jeans; the kind of effortless attire that somehow made him look like he belonged to the pages of a magazine.

"Shouldn't you be with everyone else?" she asked, her voice coming out sharper than she intended.

Jack smiled faintly, taking a step closer. "I'm not really the fishing type."

Alexa forced a laugh, but it sounded hollow even to her own ears. "You used to be."

"Things change," he said, his tone softer now. He looked at her, his gaze piercing. "Though some things don't."

Alexa felt her cheeks flush and turned back to the flower bed, pretending to adjust a plant that didn't need adjusting. "What are you doing here, Jack?"

"I think you know," he said simply.

Her hands were stilled, and for a moment, neither of them spoke. The weight of his words hung in the air, heavy and undeniable.

Later that afternoon, Alexa found herself in the kitchen, preparing sandwiches for lunch. The sun streamed through the windows, casting warm patterns on the floor, but the warmth did little to ease the chill in her chest. She could feel Jack behind her before he even spoke.

"Need any help?" he asked, his voice low and smooth.

She turned, startled to find him standing so close. His presence filled the room, making it feel smaller, more intimate.

"I'm fine," she said quickly, stepping back to put some distance between them.

Jack didn't move, his eyes fixed on her. "You've been avoiding me."

"No, I haven't," Alexa replied, though her voice betrayed her.

"Yes, you have," he said, his tone gentle but firm. "And I think we both know why."

She felt her chest tighten, her pulse quickening. "This isn't the time or place, Jack."

"When is it ever going to be the time?" he pressed, taking a step closer. "We've been circling each other our whole lives, Alexa. When do we stop running?"

Her breath hitched, her hands gripping the edge of the counter for support. She couldn't look at him, couldn't let herself fall into the gravity of his gaze.

"This isn't fair," she whispered, her voice trembling. "You can't just show up here and… and say things like that."

"I'm not the one who left," he said softly.

The words cut through her like a blade, and she turned away, unable to face the raw emotion in his voice.

That evening, as the family gathered for dinner on the porch, James couldn't shake the feeling that something was off. Alexa had been distant all week, her smiles forced, her laughter lacking its usual warmth.

He glanced across the table at her, watching as she passed a dish to Jack. Their hands brushed for just a moment, but it was enough to make James's stomach tighten.

"Alexa," James said, his voice light but probing. "Are you okay? You've seemed… distracted."

She looked up, startled, her cheeks flushing slightly. "I'm fine," she said quickly. "Just a lot on my mind."

James nodded, but he wasn't convinced. He glanced at Jack, who was listening intently to something Luke was saying, his expression calm and unreadable. There was nothing overtly suspicious about their interactions, but James couldn't shake the nagging feeling that there was more going on than Alexa was letting on.

That night, Alexa lay in bed, staring at the ceiling as James slept beside her. The sound of his even breathing filled the room, a constant rhythm that should have been comforting. But instead, it only heightened her guilt.

She thought about Jack, about the way his eyes had lingered on hers during dinner, the way his presence seemed to ignite something inside her that had been dormant for years. She hated herself for it, for letting her thoughts stray to him when James was right there, steady and unwavering.

She turned onto her side, watching James's peaceful face in the dim light. He had been a good husband, a good father. He didn't deserve this—didn't deserve her betrayal, even if it was only in her mind.

But she couldn't stop. The memory of Jack's voice, his touch, his presence—it was all-consuming, a fire she couldn't extinguish.

Unable to sleep, Alexa slipped out of bed and made her way to the porch. The night was cool, the lake was shimmering under the light of the moon. She wrapped her arms around herself, her mind racing.

"Can't sleep either?"

The sound of Jack's voice made her jump, and she turned to see him leaning against the porch railing, his hands in his pockets.

"What are you doing out here?" she asked, her voice sharper than she intended.

"Same as you, I guess," he said, his tone calm. "Thinking too much."

She hesitated, then joined him at the railing, keeping a careful distance between them. For a moment, neither of them spoke, the silence filled only by the gentle lapping of the water against the shore.

"I didn't mean to make things harder for you," Jack said softly, breaking the silence.

Alexa looked at him, her heart aching at the vulnerability in his expression. "You didn't," she said, though they both knew it wasn't true.

He turned to face her fully, his gaze intense. "I can't pretend this doesn't mean anything, Alexa. You mean something to me. You always have."

Her breath caught, her chest tightening with a mix of longing and fear. "Jack, I—"

"Don't," he said, his voice breaking slightly. "Don't say it doesn't matter. Don't lie to me, Alexa. Not about this."

She felt tears prick in her eyes, but she blinked them away, shaking her head. "It's not that simple."

"It could be," he said, his voice quiet but firm. "If you let it."

As dawn approached, Alexa returned to bed, her mind a whirlwind of emotions. She couldn't deny the pull she felt toward Jack, the way he made her feel alive in a way she hadn't in years. But she also couldn't ignore the life she had built with James, the family they had created together.

The weight of her secrets felt heavier than ever, pressing down on her with every passing moment. She knew she couldn't keep going like this, torn between two worlds, two men, two versions of herself.

But no matter what choice she made, someone would get hurt.

And as the first rays of sunlight broke over the lake, Alexa whispered into the quiet room, "What have I done?"

James woke earlier than usual the following morning, the sky still tinged with the faint glow of dawn. He lay in bed for a moment, listening to the soft rustle of the trees outside the window and the distant sound of waves lapping against the dock. Something about the stillness unsettled him.

Alexa's side of the bed was empty, the sheets cooled to the touch. He frowned, sitting up and rubbing a hand over his face. Lately, her absence seemed to be a recurring theme—not just physically, but emotionally.

He got up, pulling on a sweatshirt before heading downstairs. He found her on the porch, a mug of coffee in her hands as she stared out at the lake. Her shoulders were tense, her expression distant.

"Morning," he said, stepping outside.

She turned, startled, and forced a smile. "Morning."

"You're up early."

"Couldn't sleep," she replied, her voice light but unconvincing.

James leaned against the railing, studying her. She looked tired, as though she were carrying something too heavy to put into words. "You've been quiet this week," he said carefully. "Is everything okay?"

Alexa hesitated, her fingers tightening around the mug. "I've just been thinking a lot. Being here always does that to me."

"What are you thinking about?"

Her gaze dropped to the floorboards, and for a moment, James thought she might tell him. But when she looked back up, her smile was too bright, too rehearsed. "Just… memories. The kids growing up, summers here. It's hard to believe how much time has passed."

James nodded, though he didn't entirely believe her. "If something's bothering you, you can talk to me, you know."

"I know," Alexa said quickly. "But I'm fine. Really."

He wanted to press further, but the guarded look in her eyes stopped him. Instead, he reached for her hand, giving it a gentle squeeze. "Let me know if you need anything."

"I will," she said, her voice soft.

But as he walked back inside, James couldn't shake the feeling that whatever was bothering Alexa, she wasn't going to share it with him.

Later that morning, Alexa found herself in the boathouse, sorting through old life jackets and paddles. She had told James she was organizing supplies for the kids, but the truth was, she needed space.

The small, weathered building smelled of wood and lake water, its walls lined with fishing rods and oars. She had always loved the quiet of the boathouse, the way it felt separate from the rest of the world.

But today, she wasn't alone.

"You keep running off," Jack's voice came from the doorway, low and teasing.

Alexa turned to see him leaning against the frame, his arms crossed. He looked at ease, but there was a tension in his eyes that mirrored her own.

"I needed a break," she said simply, turning back to the shelves.

Jack stepped inside, his footsteps soft against the wooden floor. "From what? James?"

She stiffened, her hands faltering. "From everything," she said carefully.

Jack stopped a few feet away, his gaze steady. "You're good at this, you know. Pretending everything's fine. But I know you, Alexa. I know when you're not okay."

She turned to face him, her chest tightening. "What do you want me to say, Jack? That I'm confused? That I don't know what I'm doing anymore? Because I don't."

"I want you to be honest," he said, his voice soft but insistent. "With me. With yourself."

Her throat tightened, tears pricking at the corners of her eyes. "This isn't fair," she whispered.

"No, it's not," he agreed, taking a step closer. "But that doesn't mean we can keep pretending. Not after everything."

She looked away, her emotions threatening to overwhelm her. "I don't know what you want from me, Jack."

"I want you to stop running," he said, his voice breaking slightly. "Stop running from me, from us."

Alexa felt her defenses crumbling, her heart aching at the raw emotion in his words. "I don't know if I can," she admitted, her voice trembling.

"You can," he said, stepping closer until they were inches apart. "I know you can."

For a moment, the air between them was electric, charged with everything they hadn't said. But before either of them could move, the sound of footsteps outside broke the spell.

Alexa stepped back quickly, her heart racing. "You should go," she said, her voice barely above a whisper.

Jack hesitated, his gaze lingering on hers. "This isn't over, Alexa."

And with that, he turned and walked out, leaving her alone in the boathouse, her emotions in turmoil.

That evening, as the family gathered for dinner, James couldn't ignore the subtle tension between Alexa and Jack. It was in the way they avoided each other's gaze, the way Alexa's laugh seemed a little too forced when Jack told a joke.

He had known Jack for years, trusted him like a brother. But now, James couldn't shake the feeling that there was something happening beneath the surface—something he wasn't a part of.

After dinner, as the kids went off to play a board game, James pulled Alexa aside.

"Are you sure everything's okay?" he asked, his voice low.

Alexa hesitated, her smile faltering. "Why do you keep asking me that?"

"Because I feel like you're not telling me something," he said, his gaze steady.

"I'm fine," she said quickly. "Really."

James studied her for a moment, his jaw tightening. "If there's something going on, Alexa, I need you to tell me."

"There's nothing going on," she said, her voice firm but unconvincing.

He nodded slowly, though the doubt in his eyes was clear. "Okay."

But as Alexa walked away, James couldn't shake the feeling that his wife was slipping further and further away from him.

That night, Alexa stood on the dock, staring out at the dark water. The stars reflected on the surface, their light soft and shimmering. She felt the weight of her secrets pressing down on her, heavier than ever.

She thought about James, about the life they had built together, the family they had created. She thought about the stability he offered, the way he had always been there for her, even when she didn't deserve it.

And she thought about Jack, about the way he made her feel alive in a way she hadn't in years. The way his presence seemed to ignite something inside her that she thought had been extinguished long ago.

Her chest tightened as tears slid down her cheeks. She didn't know how much longer she could keep this up—this balancing act, this constant push and pull between the life she had and the life she wanted.

For years, she had convinced herself that she had made the right choice, that her sacrifices had been worth it. But now, standing on the dock with the past and present colliding around her, she wasn't so sure.

And as the night stretched on, Alexa whispered into the darkness, "What do I do?"

The water offered no answers, only the quiet lapping of waves against the shore.

The next morning, Alexa felt the heaviness of the previous night pressing down on her as she stood in the kitchen, preparing coffee. The Lakehouse, usually a sanctuary, seemed more like a labyrinth of emotions she couldn't escape. The distant sound of the kids laughing near the dock barely penetrated the cloud of tension swirling inside her.

James entered the kitchen, his presence as steady and calm as ever. But today, Alexa noticed a guard in his movements, a slight hesitation as he reached for his mug.

"Morning," he said, his voice light but cautious.

"Morning," Alexa replied, her voice barely above a whisper.

He leaned against the counter, watching her carefully. "You didn't sleep well last night."

"I just have a lot on my mind," she said, avoiding his gaze.

James studied her, the silence between them growing heavier. "You know you can talk to me, right?"

Alexa froze, her hands tightening around her mug. She could feel his eyes on her, searching for answers she wasn't ready to give.

"I know," she said finally, forcing a small smile. "I'm fine, James. Really."

He didn't look convinced, but he didn't push further. Instead, he kissed her forehead gently and left the kitchen, leaving Alexa to wrestle with her thoughts.

Later that day, Alexa found herself walking along the trail that wound through the woods behind the Lakehouse. It was a path she and Jack had walked countless times as teenagers, their laughter echoing through the trees.

She wasn't surprised when she heard footsteps behind her.

"Do you always run away when things get hard?" Jack's voice was laced with both frustration and affection.

Alexa stopped, turning to face him. He looked the same as he always had—steady, confident, and infuriatingly sure of himself.

"I'm not running away," she said defensively.

"Yes, you are," he said, stepping closer. "You've been running for years, Alexa. And now, here we are, back where it all started, and you're still doing it."

Her chest tightened, anger and guilt warring inside her. "What do you want from me, Jack? You show up here after all these years, and you expect me to just—"

"To what?" he interrupted his voice rising. "To admit that you feel the same way I do? To stop pretending this doesn't matter?"

Alexa's breath hitched, tears pricking at the corners of her eyes. "It's not that simple."

"It is," he said, his voice softening. "You're the one making it complicated."

She shook her head, turning away. "I can't do this."

Jack grabbed her arm gently, pulling her back toward him. "Alexa, look at me."

She reluctantly met his gaze, the intensity in his eyes making her heart race.

"We've wasted enough time," he said, his voice barely above a whisper. "Don't let fear keep you from living your life."

Her tears spilled over, and she pulled away, her voice trembling. "I can't, Jack. I have a family. I have responsibilities. I can't just throw it all away."

"You think I don't know that?" he said, his own voice breaking. "But what about you? What about what you want?"

She didn't respond. Instead, she turned and walked away, leaving him standing alone on the trail, his words echoing in her mind.

That evening, as the family gathered for a barbecue on the porch, James couldn't ignore the tension simmering beneath the surface. Alexa was quieter than usual, her laughter forced and her smiles fleeting. Jack, too, seemed distracted, his usual charm subdued.

As they ate, James found himself watching the two of them closely. He couldn't pinpoint exactly what it was, but there was something in the way they avoided each other's eyes, in the way their conversations felt overly polite, that set off alarms in his mind.

"Jack," James said casually, breaking the silence. "You've been spending a lot of time out here with us. Don't you have work to get back to?"

Alexa stiffened, her fork pausing midair.

Jack smiled, though it didn't reach his eyes. "I've been taking some time off. Figured I'd enjoy the peace and quiet while I can."

James nodded, though his expression remained guarded. "It's good to have you here. The kids love having you around."

Jack glanced at Alexa, his gaze lingering for just a moment too long. "I'm glad to be here."

The tension at the table was palpable, and Alexa felt like she was suffocating.

That night, Alexa stood by the window in the bedroom, staring out at the moonlit lake. James was in the shower, the sound of running water filling the room.

She felt like a stranger in her own life, torn between the safety of the world she had built with James and the fire that Jack reignited inside her.

Her mind drifted to the moment on the trail, to the way Jack had looked at her, his words cutting through the walls she had spent years building. She hated herself for wanting him, for letting her mind wander to what could have been.

The bathroom door opened, and James stepped out, a towel draped around his waist. He smiled at her, his expression soft.

“Are you okay?” he asked, his voice filled with concern.

Alexa forced a smile, nodding. “I’m fine. Just tired.”

He crossed the room, wrapping his arms around her from behind. “I feel like I’ve been losing you lately,” he said softly.

Her heart broke at his words, and she turned in his arms, placing her hands on his chest. “I’m sorry,” she whispered, her voice trembling.

He kissed her forehead, his touch gentle. “I love you, Alexa.”

“I love you too,” she replied, though the words felt hollow.

Unable to sleep, Alexa slipped out of bed and made her way to the porch. The night was cool, the stars scattered across the sky like diamonds.

She wrapped her arms around herself, her mind racing. She thought about Jack, about James, about the life she had built and the one she had left behind.

Her heart ached with the weight of her secrets, the choices she had made, and the consequences of those choices. She didn't know what the future held, but one thing was clear—she couldn't keep living like this.

As the first light of dawn began to break over the horizon, Alexa whispered into the quiet, "I have to make a choice."

And for the first time in years, she felt a glimmer of clarity.

The morning sunlight streamed through the kitchen window, spilling golden light across the countertops where Alexa stood making breakfast. She could hear James and Luke talking outside, their voices drifting in with the soft breeze. From the sound of it, James was teaching Luke how to properly cast a fishing line, and Alexa couldn't help but smile at her son's excited chatter.

But the warmth she felt for her family was overshadowed by the gnawing sense of guilt in her chest. She couldn't stop replaying her conversation with Jack the day before, his words echoing in her mind: *"When do we stop running?"*

"Mom?"

Alexa turned to see Anna standing in the doorway, her hair tied up in a messy bun and her expression curious.

"Morning, sweetheart," Alexa said, forcing a smile. "Want some breakfast?"

Anna shook her head, stepping into the room. "I was just wondering if you're okay. You seem… different this week."

The observation hit Alexa harder than she expected, her daughter's perceptiveness catching her off guard. "I'm fine," Alexa said quickly, though her voice wavered. "Just a lot on my mind."

"Is it about work? Or something else?" Anna pressed, her eyes narrowing slightly.

Alexa hesitated, her heart aching at the thought of burdening her daughter with her struggles. "It's nothing you need to worry about," she said gently, placing a hand on Anna's shoulder. "I promise."

Anna studied her for a moment before nodding. "Okay. But you know you can talk to me, right? Even if it's not kid stuff."

Alexa's chest tightened, and she leaned down to kiss Anna's forehead. "Thank you, sweetie. That means a lot."

Anna offered a small smile before heading back outside, leaving Alexa alone with her thoughts once again.

As the day wore on, James found himself watching Alexa more closely. Her distracted demeanor, her tendency to slip away from the group—it wasn't like her. He tried to brush it off, to tell himself that she was simply enjoying the solitude of the Lakehouse, but the nagging doubt in his mind refused to be silenced.

When they sat down for lunch on the porch, James caught her glancing at Jack more than once. It wasn't overt, but it was enough to unsettle him. There was something in the way she looked at him, something James couldn't quite place but couldn't ignore either.

"Alexa," James said as they cleared the table together, his tone casual but probing. "Are you okay? Really?"

She froze for a fraction of a second before resuming her task, her back turned to him. "I told you, I'm fine."

"You've just seemed… distant," he said, his voice soft but insistent. "If something's bothering you, I want to help."

Alexa turned to face him, her expression carefully neutral. "I'm just tired, James. That's all."

James studied her, his jaw tightening. He wanted to believe her, but something about the way she avoided his gaze made him doubt her words.

That night, unable to sleep, Alexa found herself on the porch once again. The cool night air brushed against her skin, and the sound of the lake was soothing in its familiarity.

She wasn't surprised when Jack appeared, his footsteps soft on the wooden planks.

"You can't seem to stay away from this porch," he said, a faint smile playing at his lips.

“Neither can you,” she replied, her voice quieter than she intended.

Jack leaned against the railing; his gaze fixed on her. “I can’t stop thinking about you,” he admitted, his voice low. “Being here, being around you again… it’s like everything I’ve been trying to forget is coming back.”

Alexa’s breath caught, her chest tightening. “Jack, we can’t—”

“Why not?” he interrupted, his tone gentle but firm. “You feel it too, Alexa. Don’t tell me you don’t.”

She looked away, her hands gripping the edge of the railing. “It doesn’t matter what I feel. I have a family. A life.”

“I know,” Jack said, stepping closer. “And I’m not asking you to throw it all away. But don’t pretend this doesn’t mean anything. Don’t pretend you don’t care.”

Tears welled in her eyes, and she shook her head. “It’s not that simple.”

“It never is,” he said softly. “But that doesn’t mean we should keep running from it.”

For a moment, they stood in silence, the tension between them palpable. Alexa’s heart ached with the weight of her emotions, torn between the life she had and the life she had always wondered about.

"I don't know what to do," she whispered finally, her voice breaking. Jack reached out, brushing a tear from her cheek. "Then let me help you figure it out."

Chapter 5

Bridgette's Legacy

The attic of the Lakehouse was a place Alexa rarely ventured into; a dusty, forgotten room filled with the relics of her family's past. It smelled of cedar and age, and the floorboards creaked underfoot as she climbed the narrow stairs. She had come up in search of an extra blanket for Luke but found herself drawn to a stack of old trunks in the corner instead.

One trunk caught her eye. It was smaller than the rest, made of worn leather with brass clasps. She didn't recognize it, which was strange—Alexa had spent countless summers exploring every nook and cranny of this house as a child.

Kneeling, she opened the trunk carefully. Inside, she found a collection of faded photographs, a silk scarf that still smelled faintly of perfume, and a bundle of letters tied with a red ribbon. The paper was yellow and delicate, the ink slightly smudged in places, but the handwriting was unmistakably her mother's.

Alexa sat back on her heels, her heart pounding. She had never known Bridgette to keep letters. Her mother had always been pragmatic, dismissive of sentimentality. Yet here, hidden away in the attic, was a treasure trove of her private thoughts.

She hesitated, unsure if she had the right to read them. But curiosity and a gnawing need to understand her mother won out. Carefully, she untied the ribbon and unfolded the first letter.

The first few lines of the letter were shocking enough to make Alexa's breath catch.

"Dearest M," it began, "I cannot stop thinking about you. Your touch, your voice—it all lingers with me, even when I know it shouldn't. I hate that I've let myself feel this way, but I can't seem to stop."

Alexa stared at the words, her hands trembling. Her mother—Bridgette, who had always been so composed, so controlled—had written this? And who was "M"?

She read on, devouring the words with a mix of fascination and disbelief. The letters painted a picture of a woman Alexa had never known, a woman who had been deeply, passionately in love with someone who wasn't her father.

In one letter, Bridgette described a secret meeting at a hotel in the city, the way her heart had raced when "M" walked through the door. In another, she wrote about the guilt that gnawed at her every time she returned home to her family, knowing she was living a double life.

"I love my children," one letter read, "but I can't pretend anymore. I've spent my life doing what was expected of me, being the woman, everyone wanted me to be. But with you, I feel alive. I feel free."

By the time Alexa finished the first few letters, tears were streaming down her face. She had always thought of her mother as cold, distant, incapable of deep feelings. But these letters revealed a woman who had been consumed by love and guilt, a woman who had wrestled with her own demons in silence.

That night, Alexa sat on the edge of her bed, the letters spread around her like pieces of a puzzle. She thought about the woman she had grown up with—the sharp-tongued, demanding mother who had always seemed more interested in molding Alexa into the perfect daughter than in understanding her.

Bridgette had never talked about love, at least not in a way that felt personal. She had given advice, of course—stern warnings about the dangers of following your heart instead of your head, about the importance of stability and practicality. But now, Alexa realized those warnings had come from a place of experience.

Her mother had known the price of passion. She had lived it.

Alexa's mind flashed to her own situation, to the fire she felt whenever she was near Jack, to the guilt that threatened to suffocate her every time she looked at James. Was she destined to repeat her mother's mistakes? Had Bridgette seen this coming, even all those years ago?

Alexa closed her eyes, letting the memories wash over her. She could almost hear her mother's voice, sharp and commanding, as it had been during so many of their conversations.

"You think love is enough?" Bridgette had said once, her eyes narrowing as she looked at Alexa. "It's not. Love fades. Passion fades. What matters is what's left when it's gone. Can he give you security? Stability? Because that's what you'll need in the long run."

At the time, Alexa had bristled at her mother's cynicism. She had been a teenager, still clinging to the romantic ideals of fairy tales and first crushes. But now, she wondered if there had been more to her mother's words than she had realized.

Bridgette hadn't been trying to extinguish Alexa's hope. She had been trying to protect herself, to spare her the pain of making the same mistakes.

As Alexa read more of the letters, she began to see eerie parallels between her mother's life and her own. Bridgette's descriptions of her affair—of the way it had made her feel alive but also hollow with guilt—echoed Alexa's feelings for Jack.

In one letter, Bridgette wrote: "I know this can't last. I know I'll have to choose between the life I've built and the life I want. But the thought of losing you feels like a death."

Alexa felt a chill running through her as she read the words. She had thought those exact same thoughts just days ago.

Her mother's affair had been a secret, buried so deeply that Alexa had never suspected a thing. But now, she wondered if it had left its mark in other ways—in Bridgette's distant demeanor, her sharp criticisms, her refusal to let herself be vulnerable.

Was Alexa destined to follow the same path? Was she already too far down the road to turn back?

The next morning, Alexa carried the letters down to the living room and spread them out on the coffee table. She stared at them for a long time, her mind racing.

James walked in, stopping short when he saw her. "What's all this?" he asked, his tone curious but cautious.

"They're my mother's," Alexa said, her voice quiet. "I found them in the attic."

James sat down beside her, picking up one of the letters. As he read, his expression shifted from curiosity to surprise to something Alexa couldn't quite place.

"She… she had an affair?" he asked finally, his voice tinged with disbelief.

Alexa nodded, her throat tightening. "I had no idea."

James set the letter down, his brow furrowing. "How do you feel about it?"

"I don't know," Alexa admitted. "Part of me is angry—angry that she kept this from us, that she lived this whole other life I never knew about. But another part of me… I don't know. I feel like I understand her better now. Maybe she wasn't as cold as I thought. She was just… hurting."

James reached for her hand, squeezing it gently. "I guess we never really know the full story about the people we love."

That evening, Alexa sat on the dock, watching the sunset. The letters were in her lap, their weight both literal and figurative. She thought about her mother, about the choices Bridgette had made and the pain those choices had caused.

And she thought about her own life, about Jack, about James, about the impossible decisions she faced.

For the first time in weeks, Alexa felt a sense of clarity. She didn't have all the answers, but she knew one thing for certain: she couldn't keep running. She had to confront her feelings, her fears, and the truth she had been avoiding.

As the sun dipped below the horizon, painting the lake in hues of orange and gold, Alexa whispered to herself, "It's time."

Alexa couldn't stop reading the letters. Each one painted a vivid picture of her mother's inner world—a woman who was not just a mother, but a person filled with longing, doubt, and a desperate need for freedom.

One letter in particular struck Alexa deeply. It was written in the aftermath of one of Bridgette's secret meetings with "M," and the tone was raw, almost frantic:

"I saw him today. He looked at me like I was the only person in the world, and for a moment, I let myself believe it was true. But when I came home and saw the children, I felt like a monster. How do you choose between the fire that makes you feel alive and the life you've built to protect the ones you love? I hate myself for wanting both. I hate myself for wanting him."

The words hit Alexa like a punch to the chest. Her mother's torment mirrored her own so precisely that it felt like she was reading a reflection of her own thoughts.

She reached for another letter, this one written years later, judging by the faded ink and worn paper. Bridgette's tone had shifted—it was calmer, more resigned.

"I told him it was over. It broke me to do it, but I couldn't keep living two lives. I chose my family, even if it means losing the part of myself that felt alive. I only hope they'll never know what I gave up for them."

Alexa's hands trembled as she set the letter down. She couldn't help but wonder if her mother had truly let go of "M," or if she had carried him in her heart for the rest of her life, a secret flame that never fully extinguished.

That evening, Alexa sat on the porch, the letters spread out on the table in front of her. The lake was calm, the water reflecting the deep oranges and purples of the sunset. She thought about her mother, about the sacrifices Bridgette had made and the burdens she had carried in silence.

For the first time, Alexa felt a pang of empathy for her mother. Bridgette's coldness, her sharp words, her insistence on practicality, it had all been a defense mechanism, a way to protect herself from the pain of what she had lost.

Alexa wondered if she was doing the same thing. Was she clinging to her life with James out of fear? Was she avoiding Jack because she didn't want to face the possibility of losing everything she had worked so hard to build?

Her thoughts were interrupted by the sound of footsteps on the porch. She looked up to see James standing there, his hands in his pockets.

"Hey," he said softly. "You've been out here for a while."

"Just thinking," Alexa replied, gesturing to the letters.

James sat down beside her, his gaze falling on the papers scattered across the table. "Still going through them?"

She nodded. "It's… a lot to process."

James reached for one of the letters, his brow furrowing as he read. "I had no idea your mom went through something like this."

"Neither did I," Alexa said, her voice tinged with sadness. "I always thought she was just… distant. But now I see it was more than that. She was carrying so much, and she didn't let anyone in."

James set the letter down, turning to face her. "Do you think she regretted it? Giving him up, I mean."

Alexa hesitated, her chest tightening. "I don't know," she admitted. "But I think it haunted her, even if she never said it out loud."

James reached for her hand, his touch warm and steady. "I'm glad you're finding this, even if it's hard. It sounds like it's giving you a new perspective on her."

Alexa nodded, though she couldn't bring herself to say what was truly on her mind, that reading the letters was also forcing her to confront her own choices in a way she wasn't ready for.

As Alexa lay in bed that night, her mind drifted back to a conversation she had with her mother years ago, during her first summer home from college.

They had been sitting on the porch, much like Alexa was earlier, watching the sunset over the lake. Bridgette had been quiet for most of the evening, her gaze distant.

"Are you happy, Mom?" Alexa had asked suddenly, the question surprising even herself.

Bridgette had turned to her, her expression unreadable. "What kind of question is that?"

"I don't know," Alexa said, shrugging. "You just seem… I don't know. Like something's missing."

Bridgette had sighed, taking a long sip of her wine. "Happiness isn't as simple as you think it is, Alexa. It's not about feeling good all the time. It's about making choices you can live with."

"What if you make a choice and regret it?" Alexa asked, her voice soft.

"Then you live with that too," Bridgette replied, her tone sharp but not unkind. "And you do your best to make the most of what you have."

At the time, Alexa had thought her mother's words were overly pragmatic, even cynical. But now, she wondered if Bridgette had been trying to prepare her for the complexities of adulthood, for the moments when love and duty would collide in ways she couldn't yet imagine.

The next morning, Alexa found herself sitting on the dock, the letters clutched in her hands. The water was calm, the sky a soft gray with the promise of rain. She heard footsteps behind her and turned to see Jack approaching, his expression cautious.

"Morning," he said, stopping a few feet away.

"Morning," Alexa replied, her voice subdued.

He gestured to the letters in her lap. "What's that?"

"Letters from my mom," she said. "I found them in the attic."

Jack sat down beside her, his gaze flicking to the papers. "Anything interesting?"

Alexa hesitated, then handed him one of the letters. "You might as well read for yourself."

He took the letter, his brow furrowing as he scanned the page. When he finished, he let out a low whistle. "I didn't see that coming."

"Neither did I," Alexa said, her voice tight.

Jack handed the letter back, his gaze softening. "What are you thinking?"

"I'm thinking that my mother and I had more in common than I ever realized," she admitted. "And that scares me."

Jack leaned forward, his elbows resting on his knees. "Why does it scare you?"

"Because I don't want to make the same mistakes she did," Alexa said, her voice trembling. "But I don't know how to avoid it."

Jack reached over, placing a hand on hers. "You're not her, Alexa. You don't have to follow the same path."

She looked at him, her heart aching at the sincerity in his voice. "But what if I already am?"

"You still have a choice," Jack said firmly. "You always have a choice."

That evening, Alexa sat alone in the living room, the letters spread out around her once again. She thought about her mother, about the choices Bridgette had made and the pain she had carried.

For so long, Alexa had been angry at her mother for the way she had treated her, for the coldness that had defined their relationship. But now, she saw her in a new light—not just as a mother, but as a woman who had loved and lost, who had made sacrifices for her family even when it broke her heart.

Alexa folded the letters carefully, tying them back together with the red ribbon. She didn't have all the answers yet, but she knew one thing for certain: she didn't want to live her life consumed by regret.

As she placed the letters back in the trunk, she whispered to herself, "It's time to stop running."

The trunk sat in the corner of the living room, its contents tucked away, but the emotional weight of Bridgette's letters lingered heavily in Alexa's chest. As the evening sun cast long shadows across the walls, Alexa found herself sitting by the window, staring out at the lake, her thoughts a tangled web of memories, realizations, and unresolved questions.

She hadn't anticipated how much her mother's letters would unearth—not just about Bridgette, but about herself. In some ways, reading those letters felt like looking into a mirror that reflected both the past and her own potential future. The fears, the guilt, the yearning—they were all there, written in ink and embedded in her own life.

James entered the room, his usual calm demeanor tinged with curiosity. He had noticed Alexa's mood shifting over the past few days, and though he hadn't pushed, the tension between them was palpable.

"You've been quiet today," he said, sitting down across from her.

Alexa looked at him, studying his face. His kindness, his steadiness, it was all still there, but so was the faint shadow of doubt she had noticed in his eyes.

"I've just been thinking," she replied softly, her voice carrying the weight of everything she wasn't saying.

"About your mom?" he asked, nodding toward the trunk.

Alexa nodded, her fingers playing with the edge of her sleeve. "She was… complicated. I always thought I understood her, but now I'm not so sure."

James leaned forward, resting his elbows on his knees. "What changed?"

"She had secrets," Alexa admitted, her voice trembling slightly. "Big ones. And reading her letter it made me realize how much I didn't know about her. About why she was the way she was."

James's brow furrowed; his concern evident. "Secrets? Like what?"

Alexa hesitated, her heart pounding. She hadn't told him the full truth about the letters, about the affair they revealed, and she wasn't sure if she was ready to. "It's hard to explain," she said finally. "But it's made me question a lot of things. About her. About myself."

James reached out, placing a hand on hers. "Whatever it is, you don't have to figure it out alone."

She forced a smile, grateful for his support but unable to shake the guilt that gnawed at her.

The next morning, Alexa found herself drawn to the dock, where the water shimmered in the early sunlight. She carried one of Bridgette's letters with her, unable to leave it behind. The words felt like a tether, connecting her to a version of her mother she was just beginning to understand.

Jack was already there, sitting on the edge of the dock with his feet dangling over the water. He glanced up as she approached, his expression unreadable.

"You keep finding me out here," she said, trying to inject some levity into her voice.

"Or maybe you keep finding me," he countered, a small smile tugging at the corner of his lips.

Alexa sat down beside him, her movements slow and deliberate. She held the letter in her lap, her fingers tracing the worn edges of the paper.

"What's that?" Jack asked, nodding toward it.

"A letter from my mom," she said, her voice quiet. "I've been trying to make sense of it."

Jack tilted his head, his curiosity piqued. "What's it about?"

Alexa hesitated, then handed him the letter. "Read it," she said simply.

Jack took the letter, his eyes scanning the page. As he read, his expression shifted curiosity giving way to surprise, then understanding. When he finished, he set the letter down carefully, his gaze meeting hers.

"Your mom had an affair," he said, his tone measured.

Alexa nodded, her chest tightening. "It changes everything I thought I knew about her. About us."

Jack leaned back; his hands braced on the dock behind him. "Maybe it doesn't change as much as you think. People are more complicated than we give them credit for. Your mom might have been cold or distant, but it sounds like she was carrying a lot. Maybe she was just trying to protect you from it."

Alexa's throat tightened, her emotions threatening to spill over. "I always thought she didn't care. But now, I wonder if she cared too much."

Jack looked at her, his expression softening. "What about you, Alexa? Are you carrying too much, too?"

She didn't answer, but the tears in her eyes told him everything he needed to know.

That afternoon, as the family gathered for lunch, James couldn't shake the unease that had been building inside him. Alexa had been distant lately, her moods shifting unpredictably. And then there was Jack—his presence seemed to amplify whatever tension lingered between them.

James watched as Alexa and Jack interacted, their conversations polite but tinged with something unspoken. He noticed the way Jack's eyes lingered on her when he thought no one was looking, the way Alexa's laughter seemed forced when he made a joke.

"Alexa," James said, his tone light but probing, "you've been spending a lot of time with those letters. Are they helping?"

She looked up from her plate, startled by the question. "I think so," she said carefully.

"What's in them?" James pressed.

Alexa hesitated, glancing at Jack briefly before turning back to her husband. "Just memories. Pieces of my mom's life I didn't know about."

James nodded, though his expression remained skeptical. “If they’re bringing up too much, you know you can take a break. You don’t have to carry it all alone.”

“Thanks,” Alexa said, her voice quiet.

But as the conversation shifted, James couldn’t ignore the nagging feeling that she wasn’t telling him the whole truth.

That evening, Alexa returned to the attic, the letters once again spread out before her. She sifted through them slowly, letting the words wash over her like waves.

One letter stood out—a final note, written in a hurried scrawl that was uncharacteristic of her mother’s usual neat handwriting.

*“To my children,” it began. “There are things I’ll never be able to explain, choices I made that I’ll carry with me to my grave. But know this: I loved you. I loved you in ways I didn’t always know how to show. And I hope that when you look back, you’ll understand that every decision I made, even the wrong ones, was because I wanted the best for you.”

Tears streamed down Alexa’s face as she read the words. For so long, she had resented her mother’s coldness, her inability to offer the warmth and affection Alexa had craved. But now, she saw it for what it was—a shield, a way to protect herself from the pain of her own choices.

Alexa folded the letter carefully, placing it back in the trunk. As she closed the lid, she felt a strange sense of peace. Her mother's story wasn't a condemnation of her own life, it was a warning, a reminder that the choices she made now would shape not just her future, but the futures of those she loved.

The next morning, Alexa sat on the porch with her coffee, watching the sun rise over the lake. The letters had given her more than just insight into her mother, they had given her clarity about her own life.

Jack appeared on the porch, his presence as familiar as the morning light. He sat down beside her, his expression quiet but expectant.

"I've been thinking," Alexa said, her voice steady. "About my mom. About the choices she made and the ones I've been avoiding."

"And?" Jack asked, his tone gentle.

"I don't want to live my life in fear," she said firmly. "I don't want to make decisions based on guilt or obligation. But I also don't want to hurt the people I care about."

Jack nodded, his gaze searching for her. "So, what does that mean for us?"

Alexa looked out at the lake, the water shimmering in the early sunlight. "It means I must figure out what I really want. Not what I'm supposed to want, but what I need to feel alive.

Jack reached for her hand, his touch warm and grounding. "You don't have to figure it out alone."

For the first time in weeks, Alexa felt a flicker of hope. The path ahead was still uncertain, but at least now, she was ready to face it.

Chapter 6

Jack's Perspective

The lake stretched out before Jack, its surface shimmering in the afternoon light. He leaned back against the porch railing, watching Alexa from a distance as she played cards with her kids on the dock. Her laughter echoed across the water, light and musical, the same way it always had.

It was a sound Jack had carried with him through decades, a sound that haunted his quiet moments and filled the empty spaces in his life.

From the outside, Jack Hayes had it all. His name graced the covers of architectural magazines, his projects reshaping skylines across the world. Clients sought him out for his visionary designs, and his financial success had afforded him the kind of life he'd once only dreamed about. But no skyscraper, no award, no amount of applause had ever filled the void Alexa Rivers left behind.

He had loved her for as long as he could remember. Even now, watching her from a distance, his chest ached with the same raw, unrelenting feeling that had gripped him since they were teenagers.

Jack's mind drifted to their first summer at the Lakehouse when they were both sixteen. It had been a summer of endless sun and stolen moments, of shared secrets and unspoken promises.

He remembered how she had looked the first time he really saw her—not just as his best friend, but as the girl who could unravel him with a single smile. Her hair had been wild from the wind, her cheeks flushed from running barefoot along the dock.

They had sat together on the boathouse roof that day, their legs dangling over the edge. Alexa had pointed out shapes in the clouds, her voice full of laughter, while Jack tried to memorize the way the sunlight danced across her skin.

"Your quiet today," she had said, nudging him playfully. "What's on your mind?"

He had wanted to tell her. He had wanted to say everything—the way she made the world brighter, the way her laugh made his chest feel too tight, the way he couldn't imagine a future that didn't include her. But the words had caught in his throat, and instead, he had shrugged.

"Nothing," he had lied.

That moment haunted him ever since. He had spent the rest of that summer trying to find the courage to tell her how he felt, but the words never came. And by the time the season ended, Alexa had fallen for someone else.

Jack's memories shifted to the night Alexa told him she was dating James. They had been sitting by the firepit, the flames casting flickering shadows across her face. She had been nervous, fidgeting with the hem of her sweater, but her eyes had sparkled when she spoke about James.

"He's… solid," she had said, her voice filled with something Jack recognized as hope. "He makes me feel safe."

Jack had nodded, forcing a smile. "That's good," he had said, even though his heart had been breaking.

He had spent the rest of the night sitting in silence, pretending to listen as Alexa talked about James. The next morning, he left the Lakehouse early, making some excuse about work back in the city. He hadn't returned for years.

The years after Alexa married James were a blur for Jack. He threw himself into his work, designing buildings that would outlast him, hoping that the weight of his ambition would be enough to drown out the ache in his chest.

His success had come quickly, each project more grandiose than the last. He became a name in the architectural world, his designs celebrated for their innovation and beauty. But no number of accolades could distract him from the fact that every woman he met fell short of Alexa.

He tried to move on. He had relationships, some lasting longer than others, but none ever felt right. They all ended the same way—with Jack realizing he was searching for something they couldn't give him.

One woman had come close. Her name was Leyla, and she had been kind, intelligent, and fiercely independent. They had dated for almost two years, and for a while, Jack thought he might be able to build a life with her. But then, one night, she had asked him about Alexa.

"You say you're over her," Leyla had said, her voice calm but edged with sadness. "But I don't think you are. I see the way you talk about her. The way you light up when you hear her name."

Jack had tried to deny it, but Leyla had been right. He wasn't over Alexa. He never had been.

Leyla had left him not long after that, and Jack had stopped trying to find someone new.

When Jack received Alexa's invitation to the Lakehouse that summer, he almost didn't go. It had been years since he had set foot there, and he wasn't sure if he could handle being so close to her again. But something inside him—hope, perhaps, or maybe just desperation—made him say yes.

Seeing her again after all these years had been both a bomb and a wound. She was older now, her features more refined, but she still had the same energy that had drawn him to her all those years ago. Her laugh still made his chest tighten; her smile still made the world feel brighter.

But she wasn't his.

Watching her with James, seeing the life they had built together, was a constant reminder of everything Jack had lost. And yet, he couldn't walk away. Not again.

That night, as Jack lay awake in the guest room, his thoughts refused to settle. He stared at the ceiling, replaying every moment he had shared with Alexa since arriving at the Lakehouse.

He thought about the way her hand had lingered on his arm earlier that day, the way her eyes had softened when she smiled at him. He thought about the tension in her voice whenever she spoke to James, the cracks in their perfect façade.

And he thought about the letter she had shown him—the one from her mother. Reading Bridgette's words had been like reading his own thoughts, the same struggles, the same guilt, the same longing.

"We've been circling each other our whole lives," he had told Alexa earlier that week. "When do we stop running?"

He meant every word. He had spent decades running—running from his feelings, from his regrets, from the life he had wanted but could never have. But now, here they were, back at the Lakehouse where it had all begun.

Jack didn't know what would happen next, but he knew one thing for certain: he couldn't keep pretending he didn't love her.

The next morning, Jack found himself walking along the shore, the cool sand shifting beneath his feet. The lake was calm, the sky a soft gray, and the world felt suspended in time.

Alexa appeared a few moments later, her steps hesitant as she joined him.

"Couldn't sleep?" she asked, her voice quiet.

"Not much," Jack admitted.

They walked in silence for a while, the tension between them was thick but unspoken.

Finally, Jack stopped, turning to face her. "Alexa, I need to say something."

She looked at him, her expression was wary but expectant.

"I've loved you for as long as I can remember," he said, his voice steady but raw. "And I know that might not change anything, but I needed you to know."

Alexa's breath hitched, her eyes filling with tears. "Jack…"

"I'm not asking you to make a decision right now," he said quickly. "I just needed you to hear it. Because if I leave here without telling you, I'll regret it for the rest of my life."

She didn't respond right away, her gaze dropping to the ground as she struggled to process his words.

"Thank you," she said finally, her voice trembling. "For telling me."

Jack nodded; his heart heavy but hopeful. For the first time in years, he felt like he had taken a step forward instead of standing still.

Jack walked the length of the shore, the lake stretching before him in calm stillness, its serenity contrasting the turmoil inside him. Each step felt heavier than the last, the weight of the words he had just spoken to Alexa pressing down on his chest. He had waited a lifetime to say them, but now that he had, the silence that followed felt more deafening than anything he could have anticipated.

In his pocket, his phone buzzed with a message, but he ignored it. His world had shrunk in the past week, folding in on itself to revolve solely around this place, this house, and her.

As his mind wandered, memories washed over him like the lapping waves at his feet.

There had been a night, years ago, when Jack had come so close to telling Alexa how he felt that the words had practically hung in the air between them.

It was the summer after college graduation, their last at the Lakehouse before their lives pulled them in different directions. The two of them had stayed up late on the dock, a bottle of cheap wine passed back and forth as they stared at the stars. Alexa had leaned her head against his shoulder, her warmth grounding him even as his heart raced.

"I can't believe this is the last summer," she had said softly, her voice tinged with melancholy.

Jack had looked down at her, his heart aching with the knowledge that everything was about to change. "It doesn't have to be," he had said, the words slipping out before he could stop them.

Alexa had lifted her head to look at him, her brows furrowed in confusion. "What do you mean?"

He had hesitated, the words on the tip of his tongue: *I love you. I've always loved you. Stay with me. Don't choose him.* But the fear of her rejection, of losing her completely, had stopped him. Instead, he shrugged, forcing a smile.

"Just that we'll always have this," he had said, gesturing to the lake, the stars, the world they had built together.

She had smiled back, her expression soft but unreadable. "Yeah," she had said, leaning her head back on his shoulder. "We will."

But they hadn't. Not really. After that summer, Alexa had thrown herself into her relationship with James, and Jack had disappeared into his work, channeling his heartbreak into blueprints and designs that kept his hands busy and his mind distracted.

As Jack stared out at the lake now, he wondered if he had built his entire life as a monument to Alexa—an empire of glass and steel to fill the void she had left behind. His success had been meteoric, but it had always felt hollow. Each award, each glowing review, had only reminded him of the one thing he couldn't have.

He thought of the women he had dated over the years, each of them kind and beautiful in their own way, but none of them Alexa. He had tried, at first, to make things work, to convince himself that he could move on. But every time he looked into their eyes, he found himself searching for her.

Even Leyla, the woman who had come closest to breaking through his defenses, had seen the truth. "You're haunted by her," she had said, her voice calm but resigned. "And I'm tired of being a ghost."

He hadn't argued. He couldn't.

When Alexa's invitation to the Lakehouse arrived, Jack had nearly deleted it without reading. The idea of seeing her again, of stepping back into the world they had shared, was almost too much to bear. But something had stopped him—hope, maybe, or stubbornness, or the quiet voice in the back of his mind that had never quite let her go.

And now, here he was, standing on the shore of the lake that had been the backdrop of their lives, his heart heavier than it had ever been.

He turned back toward the house, his steps slow and deliberate. As he approached the porch, he saw her sitting there, a book open on her lap but forgotten as she stared out at the water.

She looked up when she saw him, her expression guarded.

"Hey," he said, his voice soft.

"Hey," she replied, closing the book and setting it aside. "Did you go for a walk?"

He nodded, climbing the steps to join her. "Needed to clear my head."

"Did it help?"

"Not really," he admitted, sitting down beside her.

They sat in silence for a moment, the tension between them thick but unspoken.

"Jack," Alexa said finally, her voice barely above a whisper. "About what you said earlier…"

He turned to look at her, his heart pounding.

"I don't know what to do," she admitted, her eyes brimming with tears. "I feel like I'm drowning."

Jack reached for her hand; his touch gentle but firm. "You don't have to figure it out alone," he said. "Whatever you decide, I'm here. Always."

She looked at him, her expression filled with a mix of gratitude and anguish. "I don't want to hurt anyone."

"You're already hurting yourself," he said softly. "Maybe it's time to think about what you need, Alexa. Not what everyone else expects of you."

Her tears spilled over, and she looked away, her shoulders trembling. Jack wanted to pull her into his arms, to hold her until the weight of the world faded away. But he didn't. Instead, he sat beside her, his presence steady and unwavering.

That night, as Jack lay in bed, his mind raced with everything that had happened. He replayed Alexa's words, her tears, the way her hand had felt in his. He thought about the years they had lost, the choices they had made, and the paths that had led them back to this moment.

For so long, he had convinced himself that his love for her was a burden, something to be hidden away and carried in silence. But now, he saw it for what it was—a truth that had shaped him, guided him, and refused to let him go.

As he stared at the ceiling, a single thought echoed in his mind: *It's not too late.*

The next morning, Jack woke with a sense of clarity he hadn't felt in years. He didn't know what the future would hold, but he knew one thing for certain—he wasn't going to give up on Alexa.

As he stepped outside, the cool morning air invigorating him, he saw her standing by the dock, her arms wrapped around herself as she stared out at the water.

He approached her slowly, his steps careful but determined.

"Good morning," he said, his voice breaking the stillness.

She turned to him, her eyes tired but warm. "Good morning."

They stood there for a moment, the lake stretching out before them, the weight of their unspoken words hanging in the air.

"I meant what I said yesterday," Jack said finally. "I love you, Alexa. I always have."

She looked at him, her expression unreadable. "I don't know if I can do this," she said softly.

"You don't have to decide right now," he said, his voice steady. "But just know that whatever you choose, I'll be here. I'll wait."

Her eyes filled with tears, but she nodded, a small, tentative smile breaking through the sadness.

And for the first time in years, Jack felt a flicker of hope.

The soft ripple of water against the dock created a rhythm that matched the steady beat of Jack's heart. He lingered there after Alexa left, her figure fading into the distance as she made her way back to the house. The sunlight danced on the lake's surface, refracting into a kaleidoscope of colors that belied the storm within him.

She hadn't rejected him outright, but neither had she embraced his declaration of love. And yet, Jack felt something shift in the air between them—a glimmer of possibility, fragile and fleeting.

For years, he had carried the weight of unspoken words, of missed opportunities and unresolved longing. Now, those words were out in the open, and though Alexa's response had been uncertain, Jack knew he couldn't let fear or hesitation hold him back anymore.

Walking back to the Lakehouse, Jack's mind drifted to the years he had spent building his career. Becoming an architect had been his dream since childhood, and he had poured every ounce of himself into making it a reality. He could still remember the thrill of seeing his first design come to life—a sleek, modern structure with clean lines and open spaces, a perfect embodiment of his vision.

But with every project, with every accolade, there had been an emptiness he couldn't ignore. The more successful he became, the more glaring the absence of true fulfillment felt.

He thought about Leyla again, about how she had been the only person to call him out on his inability to let go of Alexa. It had taken him years to realize she was right. Every relationship he had tried to build had been overshadowed by the ghost of what could have been.

Now, being back at the Lakehouse, it was impossible to ignore the truth. His success had come at a cost—a cost he was only beginning to understand.

The Lakehouse itself was a place of both solace and pain for Jack. Every corner of the property held a memory—summer nights spent chasing fireflies, lazy afternoons sprawled on the dock, the scent of freshly baked blueberry muffins wafting from the kitchen.

It was here that he and Alexa had forged their bond, a connection that had grown stronger with each passing year until it became something neither of them could fully articulate.

He remembered one summer, when they were both seventeen. They had spent an entire afternoon building a treehouse in the woods, their laughter ringing through the trees as they argued over the best way to nail the planks together.

“You’re doing it all wrong,” Alexa had teased, her hands on her hips as she watched Jack struggle with a particularly stubborn nail.

“Oh, I’m sorry, Miss Expert Carpenter,” he had retorted, grinning. “Why don’t you show me how it’s done?”

She had rolled her eyes but taken the hammer from him, her movements sure and confident as she secured the nail in place.

“See?” she had said, her smile triumphant. “It’s not that hard.”

"Show-off," he had muttered, but his grin had betrayed his admiration.

It had been one of the best summers of his life, filled with moments of joy and connection that had cemented his feelings for her.

Back at the house, Jack found himself wandering into the living room, where a fire crackled softly in the hearth. James was seated in an armchair, a book in his hands, but he looked up when Jack entered.

"Hey," James said, his tone friendly but cautious. "Did you have a good walk?"

"Yeah," Jack replied, keeping his tone neutral.

The two men regarded each other for a moment, the unspoken tension between them thickening the air. James had always been polite, even kind, but Jack couldn't ignore the subtle wariness in his eyes, the same wariness that had been there since Jack's arrival.

"You've been spending a lot of time out by the lake," James said casually, though his tone carried an edge.

"It's a good place to think," Jack replied.

James nodded, his gaze steady. "I get that. This place has a way of bringing things to the surface."

Jack hesitated, unsure of how to navigate the conversation. He could feel the weight of James's unspoken questions, the doubt that lingered beneath his calm exterior.

"James," Jack said finally, his voice steady. "I don't want to overstep here, but I need to be honest. Alexa means a lot to me."

James's expression didn't waver, but Jack saw the flicker of unease in his eyes.

"She means a lot to all of us," James said, his tone measured.

"I know," Jack said. "And I'm not trying to disrupt anything. But I also think there are things she's been holding inside for a long time. Things she needs to confront."

James leaned back in his chair; his expression thoughtful but guarded. "And you think you're the person to help her do that?"

"I don't know," Jack admitted. "But I'm here if she needs me."

James didn't respond right away, his gaze fixed on the fire. When he finally spoke, his voice was quiet but firm.

"Alexa and I have built a life together," he said. "It hasn't always been perfect, but we've worked hard to make it what it is. I'm not going to let anything—or anyone—jeopardize that."

Jack met his gaze, his own resolve hardening. "Neither am I. But sometimes, we must ask ourselves if what we've built is what we really need—or if it's just what we're holding onto because it's familiar."

James's jaw tightened, but he didn't reply. Instead, he turned his attention back to his book, effectively ending the conversation.

That evening, as the family gathered for dinner, Jack noticed Alexa's quiet demeanor. She laughed at the kids' jokes and smiled at James's stories, but her heart clearly wasn't in it.

After the meal, as everyone began to scatter, Jack found her in the kitchen, washing dishes.

"Need some help?" he asked, stepping up beside her.

She glanced at him, her expression softening. "Sure."

They worked in silence for a while, the clinking of plates and the running water filling the space between them.

"Jack," Alexa said finally, her voice hesitant.

"Yeah?" She set down the dish she was holding, turning to face him. "Thank you. For being honest with me. For… everything."

He dried his hands on a towel, his gaze steady. "I meant what I said. I'll wait, Alexa. For as long as it takes."

Tears welled in her eyes, and she reached out, her hand brushing his. "I don't know what to do," she admitted, her voice trembling.

"You don't have to decide right now," he said gently. "But whatever you choose, just know that I'm here. I've always been here."

She nodded, her tears spilling over. And for a moment, they stood there, the weight of their emotions filling the space between them.

As the night settled over the Lakehouse, Jack found himself drawn back to the dock, the moonlight casting a silver sheen across the water. The house behind him was quiet now, the family having retreated to their rooms. He had excused himself after dinner, feeling the weight of the day pressing on him.

Sitting on the edge of the dock, his legs dangling over the side, Jack let out a long breath. The cool night air filled his lungs, grounding him in the moment, even as his thoughts threatened to spiral.

His conversation with Alexa replayed in his mind, her voice trembling as she admitted she didn't know what to do. It was a small moment, but it meant everything. She hadn't pushed him away—not completely. That was enough for now.

He reached into his pocket and pulled out the small leather journal he always carried. The habit of jotting down thoughts and sketches had been with him for years, a way to make sense of his restless mind. Flipping to an empty page, he began to sketch the Lakehouse as he remembered it from their teenage years—the porch where they had sat for hours, the dock where they had spent lazy afternoons, the boathouse that had always been their secret hideaway.

As the pencil moved across the page, Jack felt a strange sense of peace. The act of creating something tangible, something that connected him to the past, soothed the ache in his chest.

His mind drifted back to a memory that had been haunting him all week. It was the summer of their senior year in high school, during the annual neighborhood barbecue at the Lakehouse. Someone had set up a makeshift dance floor on the lawn, stringing fairy lights between the trees.

Jack had been standing off to the side, watching as Alexa twirled in the arms of a boy he didn't know. She had been laughing, her hair catching the light, and he had felt that familiar pang of longing that he never could quite shake.

Later that night, after most of the guests had gone home, she had pulled him onto the dance floor, her smile playful.

"Come on, Jack," she had teased. "One dance won't kill you."

He had tried to protest, but she wouldn't take no for an answer. And so, under the glow of the fairy lights, with the soft hum of music in the background, they danced.

It had been the first time he allowed himself to imagine what it might feel like to have her—to truly be with her. The memory was both beautiful and painful, a reminder of everything they had shared and everything they hadn't.

Jack closed the journal, staring out at the lake. He didn't know what tomorrow would bring, but he knew one thing: he wasn't going to let fear keep him from fighting for Alexa.

"Whatever happens," he murmured to himself, "I'm not giving up."

And with that, he stood, the quiet determination in his heart stronger than ever.

Chapter 7
The Storm

The air was thick and humid that morning, the kind of weather that hinted at an impending storm. The lake mirrored the sky, its surface an eerie, glasslike calm, and the silence around the Lakehouse felt ominous. Alexa stood by the window, her coffee cup cradled in her hands, watching as dark clouds gathered on the horizon.

"Storm's coming," James said, stepping into the kitchen and glancing at the weather app on his phone. "Looks like it's going to be a big one."

Alexa nodded but said nothing, her mind elsewhere. The tension that had been building between her and Jack all weeks felt unbearable now, like the charged air before lightning struck. She felt trapped in a web of her own making, unable to see a way out without shattering everything she had built.

The kids were excited about the storm, oblivious to the emotional undercurrents swirling around them. Anna had already gathered candles and flashlights, while Luke kept running to the dock to check on the boats, despite James's warnings to stay inside.

"Come on, Luke," James called. "Storm's about to hit. Get back in here."

As the first low rumble of thunder echoed across the lake, the family gathered in the living room, the mood light despite the tension Alexa carried in her chest.

The rain began slowly, a soft patter against the windows that quickly escalated into a torrential downpour. The wind howled, rattling the shutters, and the power flickered once, twice, before plunging the house into darkness.

"Great," James muttered, grabbing a flashlight. "Well, this is cozy."

The kids laughed; their excitement undimmed by the blackout. They lit candles around the house, their flickering light casting long shadows on the walls. The adults settled into the living room, trying to make the best of the situation.

But the storm outside was nothing compared to the storm brewing inside Alexa. She could feel Jack's presence across the room, his gaze brushing over her like a physical touch. Every glance, every movement felt charged, as if the storm had heightened the tension between them to an unbearable degree.

Later that evening, after dinner had been eaten by candlelight and the kids had gone to bed, Alexa found herself in the kitchen, staring out at the rain pounding against the windows. The house was quiet now, the only sounds were the occasional crack of thunder and the whisper of the wind through the trees.

"Couldn't sleep either?"

She turned to see Jack standing in the doorway, his figure silhouetted by the faint glow of a nearby candle.

"No," she admitted, her voice barely above a whisper.

He stepped closer, his presence filling the room. "You've been avoiding me," he said gently, but there was an edge of frustration in his voice.

"I'm not avoiding you," she said, though the words felt hollow.

"Alexa," he said, his voice soft but firm. "We can't keep pretending this isn't happening. That it hasn't always been happening."

Her breath hitched, her chest tightening as the weight of his words settled over her.

"I don't know what you want me to say," she said finally, her voice trembling.

"I want you to be honest," he said, stepping closer. "With me. With yourself."

She shook her head, tears brimming in her eyes. "This isn't fair, Jack. To James. To the kids. To any of us."

He reached out, his fingers brushing her arm. "What's not fair is lying to yourself about what you want. What you've always wanted."

The dam broke then, her emotions spilling over as she looked up at him, her tears falling freely. "I can't do this," she whispered, even as her body betrayed her, leaning into his touch.

"Yes, you can," he said, his voice barely audible. "Just this once, Alexa. Just be honest."

And then his lips were on hers, the kiss fierce and tender all at once. It was everything she had suppressed for years, every unspoken word, every longing glance, every moment of what could have been.

For a brief, dizzying moment, nothing else existed—no storm, no family, no consequences. Just them.

But then reality came crashing back.

"Alexa?"

James's voice cut through the haze like a knife, and she pulled away from Jack, her heart pounding.

"James," she said, her voice shaking as she turned to see him standing in the doorway, his expression shadowed and unreadable.

"What's going on?" he asked, his tone carefully neutral.

"Nothing," she said quickly, brushing past Jack and wiping at her tears. "I was just… I needed some air."

James's gaze flicked between them, suspicion flickering in his eyes. But he didn't push the matter, instead stepping aside to let her pass.

As Alexa hurried out of the kitchen, her guilt threatened to swallow her whole.

Left alone in the kitchen, Jack stared at the rain-soaked windows, his hands clenched at his sides. He hadn't meant for it to happen—not like that, not with so much at stake. But when Alexa had looked at him, her emotions raw and unguarded, he hadn't been able to hold back.

And now, the look on James's face was burned into his memory, a stark reminder of the lines they had just crossed.

He sank into a chair, running a hand through his hair. This wasn't how he wanted it to happen. He had always imagined a future with Alexa, but not like this, not surrounded by lies and betrayal.

For the first time in years, doubt crept into his heart. Had he made a mistake?

Alexa fled to the porch, the storm raging around her as she sank onto the steps, her hands shaking. The rain splattered against her skin, but she barely noticed. Her mind was a whirlwind, torn between the exhilaration of the kiss and the crushing weight of her guilt.

She thought about James, about the life they had built together. He didn't deserve this—none of them did. And yet, she couldn't deny the way Jack made her feel, the way he had always made her feel.

But was it worth destroying everything she had?

As the storm raged on, Alexa made a silent vow to herself: she couldn't let this continue. She had to make a choice, one way or another.

Inside, James sat in the darkened living room, the flickering candlelight casting shadows across his face. His mind was racing, piecing together fragments of the evening, the way Alexa and Jack had been avoiding each other all week, the tension that seemed to follow them everywhere, the look on Jack's face when he had walked into the kitchen.

James wasn't a man prone to jealousy, but something about the way Alexa had pulled away from him lately felt different.

He didn't want to believe it. He didn't want to believe that the woman he loved, the mother of his children, could betray him. But the storm in his heart was as relentless as the one outside, and the doubts refused to be silenced.

That night, the storm finally began to wane, the rain tapering off into a soft drizzle. But inside the Lakehouse, the tension remained, unspoken and unresolved.

Alexa lay awake in bed, staring at the ceiling as James slept beside her. She thought about the kiss, about the way Jack's touch had ignited something in her that she thought had been lost. But she also thought about her family, about the life she had built, and the sacrifices she had made to keep it together.

In the guest room, Jack stared at the ceiling, his mind replaying the moment in the kitchen repeatedly. He didn't regret the kiss—how could he, when it had been years in the making? But he hated the way it had happened, the way it had hurt Alexa, and the way it had shattered the fragile balance between them.

And in the living room, James sat alone, staring into the dying embers of the fire, his thoughts a whirlwind of doubt, anger, and sadness.

The storm had passed by the time the first rays of sunlight crept through the trees, but the atmosphere inside the Lakehouse remained heavy with tension. The scent of rain still hung in the air, mixing with the faint aroma of coffee that Alexa had brewed in the early hours of the morning.

She sat at the kitchen table, her hands wrapped around her mug, staring into the dark liquid as if it could provide answers to the impossible questions swirling in her mind. Sleep had eluded her entirely, her thoughts too loud, her emotions too raw.

Jack entered the kitchen quietly, his hair slightly tousled, his expression cautious. He hesitated in the doorway before stepping inside, the distance between them feeling insurmountable despite the intimacy of the night before.

"Morning," he said softly.

Alexa nodded, not trusting her voice.

Jack poured himself a cup of coffee and sat down across from her. For a moment, neither of them spoke, the silence stretching like a taut wire between them.

"Alexa…" Jack began, his voice low, almost hesitant.

"Don't," she said quickly, her tone sharper than she intended. She looked up at him, her eyes filled with a mix of guilt and desperation. "I can't… I don't know what to say right now."

"You don't have to say anything," Jack said, his gaze steady. "But I meant what I said last night. About how I feel. I just—"

"Jack, stop," she interrupted, her voice breaking. "Please. I can't do this."

His jaw tightened, but he nodded, leaning back in his chair. "Okay," he said quietly, his disappointment palpable.

The sound of footsteps approaching broke the tension, and they both looked up as James entered the kitchen. He stopped short when he saw them, his eyes narrowing slightly as he took in the scene.

"Morning," James said, his tone neutral but edged with something Alexa couldn't quite identify.

"Morning," Alexa replied, forcing a smile.

Jack stood; his movements deliberate. "I'm going to take a walk," he said, his voice even.

James watched him leave, his gaze lingering on the door long after it had closed.

"Everything okay?" he asked, turning back to Alexa.

"Of course," she said quickly, standing to refill her coffee. "Why wouldn't it be?"

James didn't respond, but the doubt in his eyes was unmistakable.

Jack's footsteps crunched against the damp forest floor as he made his way down the familiar trails that wound through the woods surrounding the Lakehouse. The air was cool and fresh, the storm having left the world feeling new, but the weight in his chest remained.

He replayed the events of the previous night over and over, Alexa's touch, her kiss, the way she had pulled away when James interrupted them. It had been everything he had dreamed of and everything he had feared all at once.

For years, Jack had told himself that if he could just have one moment with Alexa—one real, honest moment—it would be enough. But now that it had happened, he felt more conflicted than ever.

A part of him wanted to fight for her, to prove that what they had was worth the risk. But another part of him, the part that cared deeply for Alexa's happiness, wondered if stepping back might be the better choice.

As he reached a clearing overlooking the lake, Jack sat down on a fallen log, his head in his hands. He had spent so many years carrying the weight of his love for Alexa, and now it felt heavier than ever.

Back at the Lakehouse, James stood on the porch, staring out at the water as he sipped his coffee. He couldn't shake the unease that had settled over him since the storm. Something had shifted in the house, a tension he couldn't ignore, and his mind kept circling back to Alexa and Jack.

He thought about the look on Jack's face when he had walked into the kitchen the night before, the way Alexa had avoided his gaze. They had brushed it off, of course, but

James wasn't blind. He had seen the way Jack looked at her, the way Alexa's demeanor changed when he was around.

James wanted to trust his wife. They had built a life together, a family, a partnership that had weathered its share of challenges. But now, standing here in the quiet aftermath of the storm, he couldn't help but wonder if there were cracks in their foundation that he hadn't noticed before.

The mood in the house that day was subdued, the storm outside replaced by an unspoken one inside. The kids, oblivious to the tension, played board games in the living room while Alexa busied herself with household tasks, avoiding both James and Jack as much as possible.

By mid-afternoon, the air between the adults had grown so thick with tension that even Anna noticed.

"Is everything okay?" she asked, looking up from her game.

"Of course," Alexa said quickly, forcing a smile. "Why wouldn't it be?"

But even as she said it, she felt the weight of her own words, the lie pressing against her like a physical force.

As evening approached, James found Alexa alone on the porch, her gaze fixed on the horizon as the sun began to dip below the trees. He stepped outside, his presence drawing her attention.

“Alexa,” he said, his tone steady but serious. “We need to talk.”

She turned to look at him, her heart sinking. “About what?”

“About you and Jack,” he said, his words landing like a blow.

Alexa’s stomach churned, her pulse quickening. “What about me and Jack?”

James studied her, his eyes searching for hers. “I’m not blind, Alexa. I see the way he looks at you. The way you look at him.”

She opened her mouth to respond, but no words came out.

“Is there something I should know?” James asked, his voice quieter now, tinged with hurt.

Alexa looked away, her mind racing. She wanted to deny it; to tell him he was imagining things, but the words caught in her throat.

“James, I—”

“Don’t,” he said, holding up a hand. “Don’t lie to me, Alexa. Just tell me the truth.”

Tears welled in her eyes as she met his gaze. “I don’t know what to say,” she whispered.

His jaw tightened, his hurt giving way to anger. “That says enough,” he said, turning to leave.

"James, wait," she called after him, but he didn't stop.

As the door slammed behind him, Alexa sank onto the porch steps, her tears spilling over.

Later that night, Jack returned to the house, his footsteps heavy as he climbed the stairs to the guest room. He had spent the day wrestling with his emotions, trying to decide what his next move should be.

He couldn't keep living in this limbo, caught between his love for Alexa and the life she had built with James. Something had to give.

Sitting on the edge of the bed, Jack pulled out his journal, flipping to a blank page. He began to write, his words raw and unfiltered, a letter to Alexa that he didn't know if he would ever give her.

Alexa,

I've loved you for as long as I can remember. You've been the constant in my life, the person I've measured everything else against. But I can't keep standing on the sidelines, waiting for something that might never happen. I don't want to make your life harder, and I don't want to hurt you. But I need you to know that I'm here—not just as your friend, but as someone who believes we could have something extraordinary if we're brave enough to reach for it.

No matter what you decide, I'll always be grateful for the moments we've shared. But I hope you'll let me show you what life could be like if we stopped running from this. Yours always,
Jack

The Lakehouse was quiet, save for the occasional creak of the wooden beams as the night settled in. Alexa lay awake in bed, staring at the ceiling as the events of the day replayed in her mind. James's words echoed in her ears: *"Don't lie to me, Alexa. Just tell me the truth."*

She had never felt so torn, so utterly incapable of deciding what to do. Every path seemed fraught with heartbreak—for herself, for James, for the children, and for Jack.

Across the hall, Jack sat at the small desk in his guest room, the letter he had written to Alexa folded neatly on the table. He stared at it, his emotions swirling between hope and dread. Part of him wanted to leave it under her door, to finally lay everything bare. But another part of him knew that doing so could tear her world apart—and his along with it.

James, meanwhile, stood in the darkened living room, a glass of whiskey in his hand. He stared into the dying embers of the fire, his thoughts a storm of their own. He wanted to trust Alexa, to believe that whatever was happening between her and Jack was nothing more than old friends reconnecting. But the look in her eyes when he had confronted her earlier told him otherwise.

By the time morning arrived, the storm outside had passed, but the tension inside the Lakehouse remained. The family gathered in the kitchen for breakfast, the air thick with unspoken words.

Anna and Luke chatted about their plans for the day, oblivious to the strain between the adults. James sat at the head of the table, his movements deliberate as he sipped his coffee and flipped through a newspaper. Alexa avoided his gaze, her focus on the pancakes she was serving, while Jack remained unusually quiet, his usual easygoing demeanor replaced with a subdued intensity.

"Dad, can we go out on the lake today?" Luke asked, breaking the silence.

James glanced at Alexa before nodding. "Sure. I'll take you out after breakfast."

"What about you, Mom?" Anna asked, her tone hopeful.

Alexa hesitated, glancing at Jack before answering. "I think I'll stay back and clean up the porch. It's a bit of a mess after the storm."

"I can help," Jack offered, his voice calm but pointed.

James looked up; his gaze sharp. "I'm sure Alexa can handle it."

The tension in the room was palpable, and even the kids seemed to sense it. Anna and Luke exchanged a glance before returning to their plates, their chatter fading into an uneasy silence.

After breakfast, James took the kids down to the dock to prepare the boat, leaving Alexa and Jack alone in the kitchen.

"I shouldn't have said anything last night," Jack said quietly, breaking the silence.

Alexa turned to face him; her expression conflicted. "You didn't say anything that wasn't true."

"But maybe the truth wasn't what you needed to hear," he said, his voice heavy with regret. "I don't want to make things harder for you, Alexa."

"You're not the one making things hard," she said, her voice trembling. "This is all on me."

Jack stepped closer, his gaze steady. "You don't have to carry this alone. Whatever you're feeling, whatever you decide, I'm here. Always."

Her breath caught, and for a moment, she let herself meet his gaze, the weight of his words settling over her. But then she heard James's voice calling from the dock, and the moment shattered.

"I have to go," she said quickly, brushing past him and out the door.

Down at the dock, James watched as Alexa approached, her movements stiff and her expression guarded. He had seen Jack watching her from the kitchen window, and something inside him snapped.

"Alexa," he said, his tone low but firm. "We need to talk."

"Not now, James," she said, her voice strained.

"Yes, now," he insisted, stepping closer. "I can't keep pretending everything is fine when it's not. You've been distant, distracted, and it's not just me who's noticing. The kids can see it too."

Alexa's heart sank. "James, please—"

"Is it him?" James asked, cutting her off. "Is there something going on with you and Jack?"

The words hung in the air, heavy and unrelenting. Alexa felt her pulse quicken, her mind scrambling for a response.

"There's nothing going on," she said finally, her voice barely above a whisper.

James studied her, his eyes filled with hurt and doubt. "I want to believe you, Alexa. But you need to give me a reason to."

She looked away, unable to meet his gaze. "I don't know what you want me to say."

"How about the truth?" he said, his voice breaking.

Alexa felt tears sting in her eyes, but before she could respond, Anna and Luke called out to them, eager to get out on the water. The moment passed, but the fracture in their relationship remained.

That afternoon, Alexa found herself on the porch, staring out at the lake as the kids splashed in the water with James. Jack appeared beside her, his presence a quiet comfort.

"I talked to James," she said softly, not looking at him.

"What did he say?" Jack asked, his voice careful.

"He asked if there was something going on between us," she admitted, her chest tightening at the memory.

Jack's jaw clenched. "What did you tell him?"

"I told him there wasn't," she said, her voice trembling. "But I think he knows I'm lying."

Jack was silent for a moment before reaching for her hand, his touch gentle but firm. "Alexa, you don't have to do this alone. Whatever happens, we'll figure it out together."

She looked at him, her tears spilling over. "I'm scared, Jack. I'm scared of losing everything."

"You won't lose me," he said, his voice steady. "No matter what."

Later that evening, after the kids had gone to bed, James sat on the porch, nursing a beer as he stared out at the lake. Alexa joined him, her movements hesitant.

"Can we talk?" she asked, her voice tentative.

James nodded, though his expression remained guarded.

"I'm sorry," Alexa began, her voice trembling. "I know I've been distant, and I know I haven't been honest with you. But I need you to know that I never wanted to hurt you."

James studied her for a long moment before speaking. "Do you love him?"

Alexa's breath caught, the question hitting her like a punch to the chest. She opened her mouth to respond, but the words wouldn't come.

"That's what I thought," James said quietly, his voice heavy with sadness.

"James, I—"

"I don't need an explanation, Alexa," he said, cutting her off. "I just need to know where we go from here."

Tears streamed down her face as she looked at him, the man she had built a life with, the father of her children. She didn't have an answer—not yet.

The next morning, the Lakehouse was eerily quiet, the tension from the previous day lingering like a shadow. Alexa stood by the window, watching as James packed the car with the kids' bags, preparing to take them into town for the day.

Jack appeared behind her; his presence steady. "Are you okay?" he asked softly.

"No," she admitted, her voice trembling. "But I will be."

He reached for her hand, his touch grounding her. "Whatever you need, I'm here."

She nodded, her chest tight with emotion. The storm had passed, but the aftermath was just beginning.

Chapter 8
James's Confrontation

The house was quiet as the evening sun dipped below the horizon, casting long shadows across the porch. Alexa stood in the kitchen, rinsing the last of the dinner dishes, her hands trembling slightly under the cool stream of water. She could feel James's presence before she turned to see him.

He stood in the doorway, his arms crossed, his expression a mix of determination and sadness.

"We need to talk," he said softly, his voice carrying the weight of unspoken tension.

Alexa hesitated, setting down the plate she was holding. "Can it wait until tomorrow?" she asked, though she knew the answer.

"No," James replied, his tone firm but not unkind. "It can't."

James gestured toward the living room, and Alexa followed, wiping her hands on a dish towel. The air between them was thick, and the distant hum of the crickets outside only amplified the silence.

He sat on the edge of the couch, leaning forward, his elbows resting on his knees. Alexa sat across from him, clutching the towel in her lap like a lifeline.

"Alexa," James began, his voice calm but unsteady, "I feel like I'm losing you, and I don't know why."

Her breath caught in her chest, the words hitting her like a punch.

"What do you mean?" she asked, her voice trembling.

"You've been… different lately," he said, his eyes searching hers. "Distant. Distracted. I can see it, Alexa. I'm not imagining things."

She looked away, unable to meet his gaze. "I've just been… overwhelmed," she said weakly. "The kids, the house, everything with my mom's letters—it's a lot."

James shook his head. "This isn't just about the letters, and we both know it."

The silence that followed was deafening, and Alexa felt her heart pounding in her chest.

James leaned back, running a hand through his hair. "We've been married for fifteen years, Alexa. We've built a life together. I know things haven't been perfect, but I thought we were solid. I thought I knew you."

"You do know me," she said quickly, her voice barely above a whisper.

"Do I?" he asked, his eyes filled with pain. "Because lately, it feels like you're a million miles away."

Alexa's hands tightened around the dish towel, her guilt threatening to overwhelm her.

"Do you still want this?" James asked, his voice breaking. "Do you still want us? Because I do. I want what we have, Alexa. I want our life. Don't you?"

Her eyes filled with tears, and she looked down, unable to answer.

As James's words hung in the air, Alexa's mind began to drift to the past, to the moments that had defined their marriage.

She remembered the way James had held her after her mother's funeral, his arms steady and unyielding as she sobbed against his chest. He had been her anchor during that storm, the one person who could make her feel like everything would be okay.

And then there was the miscarriage, the devastating loss that had nearly broken her. She could still hear his voice, soft and soothing as he whispered, "We'll get through this, Alexa. I promise."

James had always been there for her, always steady, always reliable. He had given her a life of stability and comfort, a safe harbor in the chaos of the world.

But even as she thought of those moments, another image crept into her mind, Jack's face, the way he looked at her as if she were the only person in the world.

James's voice pulled her back to the present. "I need you to be honest with me, Alexa. Is there something going on that I don't know about?"

Her stomach churned, her mind racing for an answer. "James, I—"

"Please," he interrupted, his tone pleading. "Just tell me the truth."

She looked at him, her tears spilling over. "I don't know what to say," she admitted, her voice breaking.

His jaw tightened, but his expression remained calm. "Do you love me?"

Her heart shattered at the question, the simplicity of it cutting deeper than anything else he could have said. "Of course I love you," she said, her voice trembling.

"But?" he prompted, his eyes searching hers.

Alexa looked away, unable to finish the sentence.

James stood, pacing the room as he spoke. "Do you remember when we first met?" he asked, his voice quieter now, tinged with sadness.

Alexa nodded; her throat was too tight to speak.

"I was just some guy in your college lit class, completely intimidated by you," he said, a small, bittersweet smile tugging at his lips. "You were so smart, so confident. I couldn't believe it when you said yes to going out with me."

She smiled faintly, the memory bittersweet.

"I've always known I wasn't the most exciting guy," James continued. "But I thought that was what we both wanted—something steady, something we could count on. We've been through so much together, Alexa. I thought that meant something.

"It does," she said quickly, her voice cracking. "It means everything."

"Then why do I feel like I'm not enough for you anymore?" he asked, his voice breaking.

Alexa's tears spilled over, her guilt threatening to suffocate her. "James, you are enough. You've always been enough."

"Then what is it?" he asked, his tone desperate. "Because something's changed, Alexa. And I don't know how to fix it."

After James left the room, Alexa sank onto the couch, her tears coming in waves. She thought about everything he had said, the pain in his voice, the vulnerability in his eyes. He didn't deserve this—not the lies, not the distance, not the betrayal that loomed like a storm cloud over their marriage.

But then she thought about Jack, about the way he made her feel alive in a way she hadn't felt in years. The passion, the longing, the connection—it was undeniable.

How could she choose between the man who had been her rock and the man who had set her heart on fire?

As Alexa climbed into bed that night, James was already lying there, his back turned to her. She stared at the ceiling, her mind racing.

She wanted to reach out to him, to tell him everything, to apologize and promise to make things right. But she also couldn't ignore the pull she felt toward Jack, the part of her that longed for something more than stability and comfort.

She lay there in the dark, torn between the steady warmth of her husband and the fiery pull of the man who had always been in her heart.

Alexa stayed on the couch long after James had left the room, her thoughts spiraling. The confrontation replayed in her mind repeatedly, each of James's words cutting deeper than the last. She could still see the pain in his eyes, the vulnerability he rarely allowed himself to show.

The weight of her guilt pressed down on her chest like a heavy stone. James didn't deserve this. He had always been a good man—a loving husband, a devoted father. She thought about all the times he had been there for her, his steady presence anchoring her during her darkest moments.

But that didn't stop the image of Jack from creeping into her mind. The way he looked at her with such intensity, the way he seemed to understand her in a way no one else ever had—it was intoxicating and terrifying all at once.

Alexa buried her face in her hands, overwhelmed by the sheer magnitude of her emotions. She felt like she was being pulled in two completely different directions, and no matter which way she turned, someone would get hurt.

James sat outside on the porch, the cool night air doing little to calm the storm raging inside him. He had always prided himself on being a man who could handle anything but tonight had shaken him to his core.

He couldn't stop thinking about the look on Alexa's face when he had asked if she still wanted their life together. She hadn't answered, really. And that silence spoke volumes.

James took a sip of his beer, staring out at the darkened lake. For years, he had believed that their marriage was unshakable. Sure, they had their ups and downs like any couple, but he had always thought they were solid at the core. Now, he wasn't so sure.

The idea of losing Alexa was unbearable. She was his partner, his confidante, the mother of his children. They had built a life together—a life he was proud of. But as much as he wanted to blame Jack for the cracks in their foundation, James knew deep down that it wasn't that simple.

Somewhere along the way, he and Alexa had lost their connection. And if he was being honest with himself, he wasn't sure how to get it back.

As James sat there, his thoughts drifted to a time when he and Alexa had been unshakable—a time when their love had felt effortless.

He thought about the night she had told him she was pregnant with Anna. They had been sitting on the floor of their tiny apartment, eating takeout and laughing about how they couldn't afford a dining table yet. When she had slid the pregnancy test across the floor to him, his heart had nearly burst with joy.

"We're going to be parents," she had said, her eyes shining with excitement and fear.

James had pulled her into his arms, kissing her forehead. "We've got this," he had said, even though he had been just as scared as she was.

It had been one of the happiest moments of his life, and it was a memory he clung to now, desperate to remind himself of what they had built together.

Upstairs, Alexa lay awake in bed, staring at the ceiling. James's side of the bed was empty, he hadn't come to bed yet—and the silence felt oppressive.

Her thoughts were a whirlwind of guilt, longing, and confusion. She thought about the life she had built with James—the home, the family, the years of shared memories. She thought about the way he had always been there for her, even when she didn't deserve it.

But then she thought about Jack—the way her heart raced whenever he was near, the way his touch sent shivers down her spine. It wasn't just lust; it was something deeper, something she had felt for as long as she could remember.

Alexa pressed her hands to her face, tears spilling over. How had it come to this? How had she let herself get so lost?

The next morning, James woke early, having spent most of the night tossing and turning on the couch. He couldn't keep living like this, walking on eggshells around his own wife, pretending everything was fine when it clearly wasn't.

He needed answers, and he needed them now.

When Alexa came downstairs, she found James sitting at the kitchen table, a cup of coffee in his hands. His expression was calm, but his eyes were heavy with determination.

"Good morning," she said cautiously, setting the coffee pot on the counter.

"I can't do this anymore," James said, his voice steady but strained. "The silence, the distance—I can't keep pretending it's not there. Something is wrong, Alexa. And I need to know what it is."

"Do you love me anymore……"

Tears welled in her eyes, and she shook her head.

" I don't know who I am anymore!" she cried, the words bursting out of her. "I've spent so many years trying to be the perfect wife, the perfect mother, and somewhere along the way, I lost myself. And then Jack came back, and he reminded me of the person I used to be. The person I wanted to be."

James recoiled as if she had slapped him, the weight of her confession hitting him like a freight train.

"So, it is him," he said, his voice barely above a whisper.

"James—"

"No," he said, holding up a hand. "I don't want to hear it."

He stood abruptly, his chair scraping against the floor. "I need some air," he said, walking toward the door.

"James, wait," Alexa called after him, but he didn't stop.

The door slammed shut behind him, leaving her alone in the kitchen, her tears falling freely.

Later that day, Jack found Alexa sitting on the porch, her face pale and her eyes red-rimmed. He hesitated before stepping outside, unsure if she wanted company.

"Are you okay?" he asked gently.

She looked up at him, her expression filled with anguish. "No," she admitted.

Jack sat down beside her, his presence steady and calming. "What happened?"

"James and I had a fight," she said, her voice trembling. "I told him about… us."

Jack's chest tightened. "You told him everything?"

"Not everything," she said quickly. "But enough."

He reached for her hand, his touch grounding her. "Alexa, I'm so sorry. I never wanted to make things harder for you."

"It's not your fault," she said, shaking her head. "I'm the one who let it get this far."

They sat in silence for a moment, the weight of their choices pressing down on them.

Meanwhile, James stood by the edge of the lake, staring out at the water. His mind was a whirlwind of emotions—anger, sadness, betrayal. But beneath it all was a determination to fight for his family, for the life he and Alexa had built together.

He wasn't ready to give up—not yet.

James walked back to the house as the sun dipped lower in the sky, the light filtering through the trees in golden rays. The lake reflected the fading daylight, but the beauty of the scene was lost on him. His mind was heavy with the weight of Alexa's confession, her words playing on repeat in his head: *"Somewhere along the way, I lost myself."*

When had she started to feel this way? He thought back over the years, trying to pinpoint the exact moment their marriage had begun to fracture. Had it been gradual, a slow erosion he had failed to notice? Or had it been there all along, simmering under the surface until Jack's arrival brought it to a boil?

James rubbed his hands over his face, exhaustion pulling at him. He wasn't ready to let go of Alexa—not without a fight. But he wasn't sure if she even wanted him to fight for her.

As he stepped into the house, the warmth of the interior felt at odds with the chill in his chest. The kids were in the living room, watching a movie, their laughter echoing through the space. James paused for a moment, watching them, his heart aching at the thought of what all this turmoil might do to them.

Anna turned, catching sight of him. "Dad, you, okay?" she asked, her brow furrowed in concern.

James forced a smile, walking over to ruffle her hair. "I'm fine, kiddo. Just tired."

"Mom's on the porch," Anna said, her tone casual, but her eyes lingered on him as if she sensed more than she let on.

"Thanks, sweetie," James replied, kissing her forehead. "I'll go check on her."

Alexa was sitting on the porch steps, her arms wrapped around herself despite the warm evening air. She didn't look up as James joined her, sitting down a few feet away.

For a moment, neither of them spoke, the silence between them heavy but familiar.

"I'm sorry for walking out earlier," James said finally, his voice low.

Alexa glanced at him, her eyes still red from crying. "You had every right to," she said softly.

He shook his head. "I don't want to fight with you, Alexa. I just… I need to understand."

She looked down at her hands, her fingers twisting nervously. "I don't know if I can explain it," she admitted. "It's not just about you or Jack. It's about me. I've been pretending to be fine for so long, and I don't even know who I am anymore."

"You're my wife," James said, his voice breaking slightly. "You're the mother of our children. You're the person I chose to spend my life with. Isn't that enough?"

Tears welled in her eyes. "It should be," she whispered. "But sometimes, it feels like I'm just going through the motions. Like I'm living someone else's life."

James stared at her, his heart breaking. "Why didn't you tell me?"

"I didn't know how," she said, her voice trembling. "And then Jack came back, and it stirred up all these feelings I thought I'd buried. I don't even know what they mean."

James swallowed hard, his jaw tightening. "Do you love him?"

Alexa hesitated, her silence answering the question more clearly than words ever could.

Inside, Jack stood by the window, watching Alexa and James on the porch. He could see their silhouettes through the glass, the way James leaned toward her, his hands gesturing as he spoke.

Jack's chest ached with a mix of longing and guilt. He had come here hoping to reconnect with Alexa, to finally tell her how he felt, but he hadn't anticipated the fallout it would cause.

For years, he had told himself that Alexa was worth the risk, that their connection was too important to ignore. But now, watching her struggle with the weight of her choices, he couldn't help but wonder if he had been selfish to come back into her life.

"Enough," he murmured to himself, stepping away from the window.

Jack grabbed his jacket and headed for the door. He needed to clear his head, to think about what was best for Alexa—not just for himself.

On the porch, James exhaled deeply, running a hand through his hair. "I don't know what you want me to do, Alexa," he said, his voice filled with frustration. "Do you want me to fight for this? Or do you want me to walk away?"

"I don't know," she admitted, her tears spilling over. "I wish I had an answer, James. I really do."

He nodded slowly, his expression unreadable. "Then maybe we both need some time to figure it out."

"Maybe," Alexa whispered, her voice trembling.

They sat there in silence for a while longer, the tension between them thick but no longer volatile. For now, they had reached an unspoken truce and a fragile, temporary peace during the storm.

Jack wandered down to the lake, the moonlight casting a silver glow across the water. The cool night air was refreshing, but it did little to ease the turmoil inside him.

He thought about Alexa, about the years they had spent apart and the brief, electrifying moments they had shared this past week. He had never stopped loving her, but now he was beginning to wonder if his love was doing more harm than good.

As he reached the edge of the dock, Jack sat down, his legs dangling over the water. He stared out at the horizon, his thoughts racing.

"Am I doing the right thing?" he murmured to himself, his voice barely audible over the gentle lapping of the waves.

For the first time in years, Jack felt unsure of the answer.

The next morning, the tension in the Lakehouse was palpable, even to Anna and Luke. They exchanged wary glances over breakfast, their usual chatter subdued.

"Is everything okay?" Anna asked cautiously, looking between her parents.

"Of course," Alexa said quickly, forcing a smile. "Why wouldn't it be?"

James nodded, his expression calm but distant. "Everything's fine, sweetheart. Don't worry about it."

But the kids weren't convinced. Later, as they played outside, Luke turned to his sister. "Do you think Mom and Dad are fighting?"

Anna hesitated before nodding. "Yeah, but I don't think they want us to know."

"What do we do?" Luke asked, his voice small.

"I don't know," Anna admitted. "But I think we just have to wait." Alexa found herself alone in the attic later that afternoon, searching for a sense of clarity among the remnants of her family's past. She sat down on an old trunk, running her fingers over a photo album she had pulled from a dusty shelf.

The pages were filled with memories—summer barbecues, Christmas mornings, trips to the beach. There were photos of her and James on their wedding day, their smiles bright and carefree. There were pictures of the kids as babies, their chubby cheeks and gummy grins bringing a bittersweet smile to her face.

But there were also gaps in the album—moments that had gone undocumented, years that had slipped by without fanfare. Alexa wondered if those gaps reflected her own emotional distance, the parts of herself she had kept hidden even from the people she loved most.

She closed the album, her heart heavy. The choices ahead of her felt impossible, but one thing was clear: she couldn't keep living like this.

That evening, as Alexa stepped outside to clear her head, she found Jack sitting on the porch steps, his expression thoughtful.

"Hey," she said softly, her voice tentative.

"Hey," he replied, looking up at her.

She hesitated before sitting down beside him, the silence between them both comfortable and charged.

"Are you okay?" Jack asked after a moment.

"No," Alexa admitted, her voice barely above a whisper. "But I'm trying to be."

He nodded, his gaze steady. "I don't want to make things harder for you, Alexa. I just… I want you to be happy."

Her chest tightened, and she looked away, her emotions threatening to overwhelm her. "I don't know what that means anymore," she said honestly.

"Maybe it's time to figure it out," Jack said gently.

She turned to look at him, her tears glistening in the fading light. “I’m scared, Jack. I don’t want to lose everything.”

“You won’t lose me,” he said, his voice firm.

Alexa nodded; her heart torn but beating faster at his words.

Chapter 9
Jack's Plea

The morning sun filtered through the trees, casting dappled shadows along the trail that wound toward the lake. Alexa walked slowly, her steps deliberate, as if prolonging the inevitable meeting with Jack. The soft crunch of gravel beneath her feet was the only sound, aside from the gentle rustling of leaves in the breeze.

She didn't know what she would say to him—or what she wanted to hear. All she knew was that the weight of her choices had grown heavier with each passing day, and avoiding him was no longer an option.

When she reached the lake, Jack was already there, sitting on the edge of the dock with his feet dangling over the water. He looked up as she approached, his expression a mix of hope and trepidation.

"Hey," he said softly, standing as she came closer.

"Hey," she replied, her voice quiet but strained.

For a moment, they simply stood there, the tension between them palpable. The lake stretched out before them, its surface shimmering in the sunlight, a stark contrast to the storm brewing in Alexa's heart.

"I didn't know if you'd come," Jack said, breaking the silence.

"I wasn't sure if I should," Alexa admitted, her gaze fixed on the water.

He took a step closer, his eyes searching hers. "Why?"

"Because I don't know what to say," she said, her voice trembling. "I don't know what you want from me."

"What I want," Jack said, his voice firm but tinged with vulnerability, "is for you to stop running from this. From us."

Alexa's breath caught, and she turned away, her arms wrapping around herself as if to shield against the emotions threatening to overwhelm her.

"Jack…"

He stepped closer, his tone softening. "Alexa, I've loved you since we were kids. I thought I could live without you, but I can't. Every time I see you, every time I'm near you, it's like… like I can finally breathe again."

Tears welled in her eyes, and she shook her head. "You don't understand. It's not that simple."

"Isn't it?" he asked, his voice breaking. "You're not happy, Alexa. You've told me that yourself. So why are you holding on to something that doesn't make you happy?"

"Because it's not just about me!" she exclaimed, her voice rising. "It's about James. It's about the kids. It's about the life we've built together."

Jack frowned, his jaw tightening. "What kind of example are you setting for your kids if you're living a lie?"

Alexa flinched at his words, her chest tightening. "Don't you dare bring my kids into this," she said, her tone sharp.

"I'm not trying to hurt you, Alexa," he said gently. "But I need you to see this for what it is. You're teaching them that it's okay to settle. That it's okay to ignore what your heart is telling you.

Tears spilled down her cheeks, and she turned away, her hands trembling. "I don't know what to do," she whispered.

Jack stepped closer; his voice soft but urgent. "This isn't just about passion, Alexa. It's about who we are when we're together. Don't you see that?"

She turned to face him, her heart pounding as his words sank in. He reached out, his fingers gently brushing a tear from her cheek.

"You don't have to decide right now," he said, his voice barely above a whisper. "But you need to be honest with yourself. What do you really want?"

"I don't know," she said, her voice cracking. "I don't know, Jack."

His hand cupped her cheek, his touch warm and steady. "Yes, you do," he said softly. "You've always known."

Her tears came faster now, her breath hitching as she struggled to hold herself together. She wanted to deny it, to push him away, but she couldn't. The truth was there, undeniable and inescapable.

As the sun began to dip lower in the sky, casting a golden glow over the lake, Jack stepped back, giving her space.

"If you stay," he said quietly, "I'll let you go. I won't push anymore. But if you leave…"

He paused, his gaze steady. "If you leave, I'll be waiting."

Alexa stared at him, her heart breaking under the weight of his words. She didn't know how to respond, didn't know how to navigate the storm of emotions swirling inside her.

Jack turned and began to walk away, his footsteps slow and deliberate.

"Jack," she called after him, her voice trembling.

He stopped but didn't turn around.

"I'm sorry," she said, her voice barely audible.

He nodded, his shoulders slumping slightly, and continued walking until he disappeared into the trees.

Alexa stood there on the dock long after Jack had gone, her mind racing. The lake stretched out before her, calm and serene, a stark contrast to the chaos inside her.

She thought about James, about the life they had built together. She thought about their children, their home, the years of memories they had shared. She thought about the times James had been her rock, the steady presence she could always count on.

But then she thought about Jack. She thought about the way he made her feel alive, the way he looked at her like she was the only person in the world. She thought about the years they had lost, the love that had always lingered between them, unspoken but undeniable.

How could she choose between the man who had been her foundation and the man who had always held her heart?

That night, Alexa lay awake in bed, staring at the ceiling as James slept beside her. She could hear his steady breathing, could feel the warmth of his body next to hers. But her mind was elsewhere, replaying her conversation with Jack repeatedly.

His words echoed in her head: "If you leave, I'll be waiting."

Alexa felt like she was being torn in two, her heart and her mind pulling her in opposite directions. She wanted to stay, to hold on to the life she had built with James. But she also couldn't ignore the part of her that longed for Jack, that craved the passion and connection she had never truly found with anyone else.

She closed her eyes, wanting herself to sleep, but the tears came instead, silent and relentless.

The next morning, James watched Alexa carefully as they ate breakfast. She was quieter than usual, her movements slower, her gaze distant.

"Alexa," he said gently, setting down his coffee cup.

She looked up at him, her eyes red and tired.

"Are you okay?" he asked, his voice filled with concern.

She hesitated before nodding. "I'm fine," she said, though her voice lacked conviction.

James didn't press her, but he could feel the growing distance between them, the chasm that seemed to widen with each passing day.

As the day went on, Alexa found herself retreating to the attic, the one place in the house where she could truly be alone. She sat by the window, staring out at the lake as she wrestled with her thoughts.

Jack's words echoed in her mind, along with James's pleas for honesty. She knew she couldn't keep living like this, caught between two worlds, two lives, two loves.

But no matter which path she chose, someone would get hurt.

And for the first time in her life, Alexa didn't know if she was strong enough to make the choice.

After spending most of the morning in the attic, Alexa finally descended, her heart still heavy from her conversation with Jack. The house was quiet—too quiet. James had taken the kids out for the day, leaving her alone with her thoughts. Normally, she would have relished the solitude, but today it felt like a prison.

She wandered into the kitchen, the echoes of Jack's words still reverberating in her mind. *"If you stay, I'll let you go. But if you leave, I'll be waiting."*

His voice had been raw, filled with a vulnerability that shook her to her core. She thought about the way he had looked at her, as if she were the only thing that mattered in the world. And then she thought about James, the steady, reliable presence who had been her partner for so many years.

Alexa leaned against the counter, her head in her hands. How could she possibly choose between the man who had been her rock and the man who had set her heart on fire?

The lake called to her again, its calm surface a cruel contrast to the storm inside her. Alexa found herself drawn to the path leading down to the water, her steps slow and measured.

As she walked, memories of her mother, Bridgette, came flooding back. She could almost hear her voice—sharp, commanding, yet filled with an undercurrent of wisdom.

"Life is full of choices, Alexa," Bridgette had once said. "But you can't live your life making decisions that only make other people happy. At some point, you must ask yourself what *you* want."

Alexa had been in her early twenties when her mother had said that, and at the time, she had dismissed it as one of Bridgette's many cryptic musings. But now, those words felt heavier, more relevant than ever.

She reached the dock and sat down, her legs dangling over the edge as she stared at the water. The lake had always been her sanctuary, but now it felt like it was mocking her, its stillness a reminder of the chaos she couldn't escape.

The sound of footsteps behind her made her turn. Jack stood at the edge of the trail, his expression unreadable.

"I thought you might be here," he said softly, stepping onto the dock.

Alexa turned back to the water, her heart pounding in her chest. She didn't have the energy for another confrontation, but part of her was glad he had come.

"Shouldn't you be somewhere else?" she asked, her tone tinged with exhaustion.

"Probably," Jack admitted, sitting down beside her. "But I couldn't leave things like they were this morning."

She sighed, her shoulders slumping. "What do you want me to say, Jack?"

"I don't want you to say anything," he said. "I just want you to listen."

He paused, gathering his thoughts. "Alexa, I know this isn't easy for you. And I'm not here to make it harder. But I need you to know something."

She glanced at him, her breath catching at the intensity in his eyes.

"I'm not asking you to choose me because I think it'll be easy," he continued. "I'm asking you to choose me because I believe in what we have. Because I believe in *us*."

Tears welled in her eyes, and she looked away, her gaze fixed on the horizon.

"Do you know what it's been like for me all these years?" Jack asked, his voice breaking. "Watching you build a life with someone else? Telling myself I didn't deserve you that you were better off without me? It's been hell, Alexa. And the worst part is, I can't stop loving you. I've tried. God, I've tried. But I can't."

Her tears spilled over, and she shook her head. "Jack, please. Don't do this."

"I have to," he said firmly. "Because if I don't, I'll regret it for the rest of my life."

Alexa buried her face in her hands, her sobs shaking her shoulders. "I don't know what to do," she admitted, her voice muffled.

Jack reached out, his hand gently resting on her back. "Yes, you do," he said softly. "You're just afraid to admit it."

She lifted her head, her tear-streaked face turning toward him. "What if I make the wrong choice?"

"Then we figure it out together," he said simply. "I'm not promising it'll be perfect, Alexa. But I am promising it'll be real."

Her heart ached at his words, the sincerity in his voice cutting through her defenses.

Without thinking, Alexa leaned forward, her lips brushing against his. The kiss was soft at first, hesitant, but it quickly deepened, years of longing and suppressed desire spilling over.

Jack cupped her face in his hands, his gentle touch yet firm, as if he were afraid she might pull away. But she didn't. In that moment, nothing else mattered—no responsibilities, no consequences, no guilt.

When they finally pulled apart, Alexa's breath was ragged, her chest heaving. "I can't keep doing this," she whispered.

"Then don't," Jack said, his forehead resting against hers. "Choose me, Alexa. Please."

The weight of his plea hung in the air as they sat there, their hands intertwined. Alexa's mind raced, her emotions a whirlwind of love, guilt, and fear. She wanted to say yes, to give herself permission to follow her heart. But the thought of leaving James, of breaking apart her family, felt like an insurmountable obstacle.

"I need time," she said finally, her voice barely audible.

Jack nodded, though the pain in his eyes was evident. "I'll wait," he said. "But not forever."

Alexa swallowed hard, her throat tight with emotion. "I'm sorry," she whispered.

"Don't be," Jack said softly. "Just… don't let fear keep you from being happy."

As Alexa walked back to the house, her heart heavy, Jack remained on the dock, staring out at the water. Meanwhile, James stood by the living room window, watching her approach.

He had returned home early, hoping to surprise her, but instead, he had seen her walking back from the lake—alone but visibly shaken.

James's stomach churned with unease. He didn't know what had happened at the lake, but he could feel the growing distance between them like a physical barrier.

When Alexa stepped inside, she froze at the sight of him. "James," she said, her voice tinged with surprise.

"You were out?" he asked, his tone carefully neutral.

"Just went for a walk," she said quickly, avoiding his gaze.

James nodded, though his eyes lingered on her for a moment longer than necessary. "Dinner's almost ready," he said, turning toward the kitchen.

"Okay," Alexa replied, her voice quiet.

As she followed him, the weight of her secrets pressed down on her, and she wondered how much longer she could keep pretending everything was fine.

The family sat around the table that evening, the conversation light but forced. Anna and Luke talked about their day, their laughter ringing hollow in Alexa's ears. James remained unusually quiet, his gaze flicking toward Alexa every so often.

When dinner was over, Alexa retreated to the bedroom, her mind racing. She sat on the edge of the bed, staring at the floor, her hands twisting nervously in her lap.

She thought about Jack, about his words, his touch, his kiss. She thought about James, about the life they had built together, the promises they had made.

And for the first time, Alexa realized she couldn't have both.

After dinner, Alexa retreated to the small sitting room at the back of the house, away from the noise of the television where James and the kids were watching a movie. She needed the space to think, to unravel the mess of emotions that had taken hold of her heart.

The room was quiet, saved for the rhythmic ticking of the antique clock on the wall. Alexa sat by the window, the night cloaking the lake in darkness. Her reflection stared back at her, fragmented by the faint streaks on the glass.

She replayed her conversation with Jack at the lake—the intensity in his voice, the rawness of his plea. She had kissed him, let herself get swept away by the emotions she'd fought so hard to suppress. And yet, even now, the memory of it stirred something inside her, a deep, aching desire that refused to be silenced.

But with that desire came an equal measure of guilt. She thought of James, of his quiet presence and unwavering support, of the life they had built together. Was it worth risking all of that for a chance at something that might not last?

The questions circled endlessly in her mind, leaving her drained and no closer to an answer.

Hours later, when Alexa finally joined James in the bedroom, she found him already lying in bed, his hands clasped behind his head as he stared at the ceiling.

"You, okay?" he asked, his tone casual but tinged with concern.

"Yeah," Alexa replied, though the words felt hollow.

"You seemed… distant at dinner," he said, his eyes flicking toward her.

"I've just had a lot on my mind," she said, pulling back the covers and sliding into bed beside him.

James studied her for a moment before nodding. "I get it. But if you ever want to talk, I'm here."

"Thanks," Alexa said softly, though her chest tightened at the thought.

As James rolled onto his side and drifted off to sleep, Alexa lay awake, her mind restless. She knew James could sense that something was off, but she wasn't ready to confront him—not yet.

At the same time, Jack sat on the edge of his bed in the guest room, his hands resting on his knees. He stared at the floor, his thoughts heavy with the weight of everything he had said to Alexa earlier.

He had put his heart on the line, laid everything bare, and now the waiting was unbearable. He had told her he would let her go if she chose to stay, but the thought of never seeing her again, of never knowing what it could have been, filled him with a sense of loss so profound it was almost physical.

For years, Jack had convinced himself that he could live without Alexa—that he could bury his feelings and move on. But seeing her again, being near her, had brought everything rushing back. And now, he couldn't imagine going back to the life he had before.

He sighed, running a hand through his hair. No matter what happened, he had no regrets about telling her more than once how he felt. At least now, she knew the truth.

The following morning, the atmosphere in the Lakehouse was strained, the unspoken tension hanging over everyone like a fog. Alexa moved through the motions of making breakfast, her movements robotic as her mind remained elsewhere.

James sat at the table, reading the newspaper, his face unreadable. Anna and Luke chatted about their plans for the day, oblivious to the underlying currents in the room.

When Jack walked into the kitchen, Alexa felt her pulse quicken. She avoided his gaze, focusing intently on flipping pancakes as if her life depended on it.

"Morning," Jack said, his voice calm but deliberate.

"Morning," James replied, glancing up briefly.

Alexa mumbled a quiet "Good morning" without looking up.

Jack poured a cup of coffee for himself and leaned against the counter, his eyes flicking between Alexa and James. The silence was uncomfortable, and even the kids seemed to sense it.

"Can we go to the lake today, Dad?" Luke asked, breaking the tension.

James folded the newspaper and set it aside. "Sure. Why not?"

"Can Uncle Jack come too?" Anna asked brightly, her question hanging in the air.

Alexa froze, her heart racing.

James's gaze shifted to Jack, his expression unreadable. "What do you say, Jack? Feel like spending some time on the water?"

Jack hesitated, his eyes flicking briefly to Alexa before settling on James. "Sure," he said finally, forcing a smile. "Sounds good."

An hour later, the family was out on the lake, the tension between the adults palpable despite the bright, sunny day. Anna and Luke sat at the bow of the boat, their laughter carrying across the water as they dipped their hands into the cool surface.

James steered the boat with practiced ease, his gaze fixed on the horizon. Alexa sat beside him, her hands resting in her lap, her posture stiff. Jack sat across from her, his expression calm but distant.

"So, Jack," James said after a long silence, his tone casual but with an edge of curiosity. "What's your plan after this? Heading back to the city?"

"Eventually," Jack replied, his gaze steady. "But I haven't decided how soon."

James nodded, his eyes narrowing slightly. "Must be nice, having that kind of flexibility."

"It has its perks," Jack said, his tone measured.

Alexa shifted uncomfortably, her fingers twisting together. The tension between the two men was subtle but unmistakable, their words laced with an undercurrent of challenge.

Later that afternoon, while James and the kids were swimming near the dock, Alexa found herself alone with Jack on the porch. She had been avoiding him all day, but now there was no escaping the inevitable conversation.

"You've been quiet," Jack said, breaking the silence.

"I've had a lot to think about," Alexa admitted, her voice soft.

He asked, "About us?" His tone was gentle but insistent.

Alexa sighed, leaning against the railing. "About everything."

Jack stepped closer, his gaze searching for hers. "Alexa, I know this isn't easy. But you must make a choice. You can't keep living in limbo."

"I know," she said, her voice barely above a whisper.

"Do you?" he asked, his tone sharper than before. "Because it doesn't feel like you do. It feels like you're trying to have it both ways."

His words stung, but she knew he was right. She turned to face him, her eyes filled with tears. "I'm scared, Jack. I'm scared of making the wrong choice. Of hurting the people, I love."

"You're already hurting them," he said softly. "And you're hurting yourself."

From the water, James watched the exchange between Alexa and Jack, his chest tightening. He couldn't hear what they were saying, but the closeness between them, the intensity of their conversation, was undeniable.

A part of him wanted to march up there and demand answers, to finally confront Alexa and Jack about what was going on. But another part of him was afraid of what he might hear.

He turned his attention back to the kids, forcing a smile as they splashed around, but the unease in his heart refused to subside.

That evening, after the kids had gone to bed, Alexa sat alone in the living room, her heart heavy. She thought about Jack's words, about the life he was offering her, the chance to finally follow her heart.

But she also thought about James, about the man who had stood by her through everything, who had given her a life of stability and comfort.

Tears streamed down her face as she realized there was no easy answer. No matter what she chose, someone would get hurt—and so would she.

Chapter 10
The Breaking Point

The air in the Lakehouse was heavy with anticipation as the family gathered around the large dining table for the farewell dinner. The extended family had spent the week enjoying the beauty of the lake and the warmth of the house, but tonight, the atmosphere was different. The laughter felt strained, the conversations muted.

Alexa sat at the table; her hands folded tightly in her lap. She had spent the day trying to convince herself that she could get through the evening without everything unraveling. But the pressure had been building for weeks, and she could feel the cracks widening.

James sat at the head of the table, his gaze sweeping over the guests. His usual warmth was tempered by a quiet intensity that Alexa couldn't ignore. Jack was seated on the opposite side of the table, his presence like a live wire. Every time their eyes met; Alexa felt a jolt of electricity she couldn't suppress.

The children, oblivious to the undercurrents, laughed and joked with their cousins, their joy a stark contrast to the tension between the adults.

As the dinner progressed, James raised his glass, smiling faintly. “To family,” he said, his voice steady but lacking its usual warmth. “And to the memories we’ve made here.”

The guests raised their glasses, murmuring their agreements, but Alexa could feel the weight of his words. She glanced at him, catching the flicker of something in his eyes, an accusation, a plea, or perhaps both.

The meal continued, but the tension only grew. At one point, James made an off-hand comment about trust, his tone light but his words sharp. “It’s funny,” he said, smiling as he passed a dish to Alexa, “how trust can be the foundation of everything—or the thing that tears it all apart.”

Alexa froze, her hand trembling slightly as she took the dish. She could feel Jack’s gaze on her, his discomfort palpable.

“James,” she said softly, her voice strained.

“What?” he replied, his tone casual. “Just making an observation.”

The conversation around the table faltered, the laughter dying down as the guests sensed the shift in tone. Alexa felt like the walls were closing in around her, the weight of her secrets suffocating.

The breaking point came when James set down his fork, his gaze fixed firmly on Alexa.

"Alexa," he said, his voice low but firm. "Are you still here with me, or are you somewhere else?"

The table fell silent, all eyes turning to Alexa. Her chest tightened, her pulse quickening as she struggled to find her voice.

"I—" she began, but the words caught in her throat.

"Because if you're not," James continued, his tone unrelenting, "I think I deserve to know."

The room was deathly quiet, the tension thick enough to cut with a knife. Alexa could feel the weight of everyone's stares, the unspoken questions hanging in the air.

"I need a moment," she said finally, her voice trembling. She stood abruptly, her chair scraping against the floor, and hurried out of the room.

Alexa stepped out onto the porch, the cool evening air hitting her like a slap. She leaned against the railing, her breaths coming in shallow gasps as tears streamed down her face.

She heard the door creak open behind her, and she didn't need to turn to find out who it was.

"Alexa," Jack said softly, his voice filled with concern.

"Don't," she said, her voice breaking. "I can't do this right now."

He stepped closer, his presence steady but not imposing. "You don't have to do it alone," he said gently.

She turned to face him, her expression raw with pain. "I don't know how to choose without breaking everything," she admitted, her voice trembling. "James, the kids… they don't deserve this."

Jack reached out, his hand brushing her cheek. "And what about you?" he asked, his voice filled with quiet desperation. "What do you deserve?"

Her breath hitched, and for a moment, she couldn't speak.

"This isn't just about passion, Alexa," Jack continued. "It's about who you are. Who we are—together."

Tears spilled over her cheeks, and she shook her head. "I'm so scared, Jack. What if I make the wrong choice?"

He leaned closer, his forehead resting gently against hers. "I'd wait forever if it meant you'd choose me," he whispered, his voice barely audible.

The kiss that followed wasn't like the ones they had shared before. It wasn't fueled by passion or longing, but by something deeper—an unspoken understanding of everything that had led them to this moment.

When they pulled apart, Alexa's tears flowed freely. "I don't know if I can do this," she admitted.

"You can," Jack said, his voice steady. "But whatever you decide, make sure it's what you really want."

When Alexa returned inside, her heart heavy with the weight of her emotions, she found James waiting for her in the living room. The rest of the family had moved to the back patio, the noise of their laughter filtering faintly through the house.

James stood as she entered, his expression calm but resigned.

"Alexa," he said quietly, his voice free of anger or accusation.

She stopped in her tracks, her breath catching in her chest.

"I'm not going to push you," he continued. "But I need to know one thing: whatever you decide, is it real? Is it what you truly want?"

Her tears welled up again, and she nodded slowly. "I don't want to hurt you, James. I never wanted this."

"I know," he said, his voice soft but steady. "But here we are."

They stood there in silence, the weight of everything unsaid hanging between them.

Later that evening, the family gathered around the firepit for one last night together. Alexa sat with the kids; her arms wrapped around them as they roasted marshmallows. James sat a few feet away, his expression thoughtful as he watched his family.

Jack lingered on the outskirts, his presence both comforting and painful for Alexa. She could feel his eyes on her, his silent support, a reminder of everything they had shared that evening.

The kids laughed and chatted, oblivious to the emotional undercurrents. But Alexa knew that this fragile moment of peace couldn't last. A decision had to be made, and soon.

The long wooden table in the Lakehouse dining room was adorned with candles and bowls of freshly prepared food. The room should have felt warm and inviting, but to Alexa, it was suffocating. The extended family chatted and laughed, their voices rising and falling like waves, but she could hardly focus. Her hands trembled as she passed a dish of roasted vegetables, her chest tightening with every glance James sent her way.

He hadn't said much during the meal, but his silence spoke volumes. His usual easy smile was gone, replaced by a faint crease in his brow and a distant look in his eyes. She knew he was watching her, piecing together the fragments of her distraction, her distance, and the way her gaze.

The conversation resumed, but the tension didn't dissipate. Alexa tried to engage with the family, forcing herself to laugh at their jokes and nod at their stories, but her heart wasn't in it. She felt like she was drowning, every moment stretching unbearably.

Jack stepped closer. Tears welled in her eyes, and she shook her head. "I don't know how to choose without breaking everything."

Jack's gaze softened, and he reached for her hand, his touch warm and grounding. "Alexa, you're not breaking everything. You're trying to find yourself again. And that's not something to feel guilty about."

"I feel like I'm drowning," she whispered, her tears spilling over. "I can't keep living like this, but I don't know how to stop."

Jack cupped her face gently, his thumbs brushing away her tears. "You don't have to have all the answers right now," he said softly. "But I need you to know something. This isn't just about passion for me. It's about who I am when I'm with you. It's about what we could be, together."

Her breath hitched, her heart aching at the raw emotion in his voice.

"I'd wait forever if it meant you'd choose me," he whispered, his lips brushing against hers in a kiss that was filled not with urgency but with longing and tenderness.

When Alexa returned inside, her face still streaked with tears, the dining room was quiet. The extended family had dispersed into other parts of the house, leaving James alone at the table.

He looked up as she entered, his expression calm but heavy with resignation.

"James," she began, her voice trembling.

He held up a hand, stopping her. "You don't have to explain," he said quietly. "I think I already know."

She stood there, her chest tightening as she waited for him to say more.

"I said this before, I just need to know one thing," he said, his voice steady despite the pain in his eyes. "Whatever you decide, is it real? Is it what you truly want?"

Tears filled her eyes again, and she nodded. "I don't know how to answer that yet," she admitted.

James's gaze lingered on her for a moment before he stood, his movements deliberate. "When you figure it out," he said, his voice softer now, "I'll be here. Or I won't. But either way, I need you to be honest—with me, with yourself, and with the kids."

Alexa's breath caught as he walked past her, his presence steady even as the distance between them grew.

As the room emptied, only James, Jack, and the hum of tension remained.

Once they were alone, James stood, his movements deliberate. He picked up his wine glass, swirling the deep red liquid before taking a slow sip. Then, without looking at Jack, he spoke.

"You've been quiet all evening," James said, his tone calm but edged with something sharp.

Jack met his gaze, his eyes steady. "Not much to say, I suppose."

James gave a bitter chuckle, setting the glass down with a soft clink. "Isn't there?" he asked, finally looking directly at Jack.

Jack felt the weight of James's scrutiny, but he didn't flinch. "If you have something to say, James, just say it."

James exhaled his nose, leaning against the back of his chair. "I'm not blind, Jack. I see the way you look at her."

Jack's heart pounded, but he kept his composure. "And how do I look at her?"

"Like she's the answer to every question you've ever had," James said flatly. "And maybe she is. But what I need to know is whether she's asking herself the same question about you."

Jack hesitated, unsure how to respond. He wasn't ready to lie, but the truth would only fan the flames.

"She's not something you can win, James," Jack said carefully. "She's a person. A woman trying to figure out what she wants."

"And you think it's you," James countered, his voice dropping lower.

"I don't know what she'll decide," Jack admitted. "But I love her. I've always loved her."

James flinched, the words striking like a blow. For a moment, the only sound was the wind outside, rustling the trees.

"You're a bold man, Jack," James said finally, his voice quiet but firm. "But let me make one thing clear. If she chooses me—and I think there's a good chance, she will—you need to let her go. Completely."

Jack nodded, though the weight of James's words settled heavily in his chest. "And if she doesn't?"

James stared at him for a long moment, his face unreadable. Then, without another word, he turned and walked away.

That night, Alexa lay awake in bed, her thoughts spinning. James's words echoed in her mind: *"Whatever you decide, is it real?"*

She thought about Jack, about the way he made her feel alive, the way his touch set her heart racing. She thought about the kiss they had shared on the porch, the quiet desperation in his voice as he told her he would wait for her.

But she also thought about James—their years together, their shared history, the life they had built. She thought about the way he had always been there for her, his unwavering support even now, when she had given him every reason to walk away.

The weight of her choices pressed down on her like a physical force, and for the first time, Alexa realized there was no path forward that wouldn't leave someone hurt.

Alexa stood at the edge of the lake; her arms wrapped around herself as the cool night air bit her skin. The moon hung low in the sky, its reflection rippling across the dark water.

She heard Jack's footsteps before she saw him, his slow, measured pace signaling his reluctance to intrude.

"Alexa," he said softly, stopping a few feet away.

She didn't turn to face him. "You shouldn't be here."

"I know," he admitted, his voice gentle. "But I couldn't let you go through this alone."

Tears spilled down her cheeks, and she wiped them away quickly, as if trying to erase the evidence of her pain. "I don't know how to do this, Jack," she said, her voice trembling. "I don't know how to choose without breaking everything."

He stepped closer, his hands resting lightly on her arms. "It's okay to be scared," he said. "But you don't have to figure it all out tonight. Just tell me what you feel—right here, right now."

Alexa turned to face him, her tears glistening in the moonlight. "I feel like I'm drowning," she admitted. "I love my family, Jack. I love James. But with you… it's different. It's like I can finally breathe, and I don't know what to do with that."

Jack's own eyes glistened with unshed tears as he reached up to cup her face. "This isn't about breaking anyone, Alexa. It's about building something real. Something that makes you happy."

He leaned forward, his lips brushing against hers in a kiss that wasn't about passion but about longing—about all the moments they had missed and the future they both feared might never come.

When they pulled apart, Jack whispered, “I said it before I’d wait forever if it meant you’d choose me.”

Alexa stood by the lake long after Jack left, the chill in the air doing little to soothe the storm inside her. When she finally made her way back to the house, her steps were slow and hesitant.

James was waiting for her in the living room, sitting in his favorite chair with a glass of whiskey in hand. He looked up as she entered, his expression calm but heavy with resignation.

“Did you get some air?” he asked, his tone even.

Alexa nodded, unable to meet his gaze.

James set his glass down on the table beside him and leaned forward, his elbows resting on his knees. “I’m not going to ask where you were,” he said. “And I’m not going to ask who you were with. I think we both know the answers.”

Her breath hitched, and she wrapped her arms around herself. “James, I—”

He held up a hand, stopping her. “I don’t need an explanation, Alexa. What I need is the truth.”

She swallowed hard, her tears threatening to spill over.

“Whatever you decide,” James said quietly, “I just need to know it’s real. Not for me. Not for Jack. For you.”

Alexa's tears fell freely now, her heart breaking under the weight of his words. She wanted to speak, to give him the answers he deserved, but all she could do was nod.

That night, the Lakehouse was silent. Alexa lay awake in bed, staring at the ceiling as James slept beside her, his breathing slow and steady. Across the hall, Jack sat by the window in his guest room, staring out at the darkened lake.

Each of them was caught in their own storm, grappling with love, loyalty, and the weight of impossible choices.

Alexa knew the time to avoid the truth had passed. The breaking point had arrived, and whatever came next would change everything.

Alexa stood on the porch; her breath shake as she tried to process everything that had happened at the dinner table. The echo of James's voice—his direct, searing question—still rang in her ears. *"Are you still here with me, or are you somewhere else?"*

The weight of the question wasn't just in the words themselves, but in the vulnerability behind them. James was a man who rarely asked for reassurance. He had always been steady, certainly, the kind of person who would quietly endure hardship without complaint. But tonight, he had reached his limit.

The cool night air brushed against her skin, but it did little to calm the storm inside her. The quiet hum of the lake, usually a soothing balm, felt deafening now. She felt the pressure of Jack's presence before she turned to see him standing just a few feet away, his face shadowed by the dim porch light.

"You shouldn't have followed me," Alexa said softly, though her voice lacked conviction.

"I couldn't stay inside," Jack replied, stepping closer. "Not after that."

His words were gentle, but Alexa heard the underlying urgency in them. He was giving her space, yes, but it was clear he was also hoping—praying—for some kind of clarity.

"Jack, this is…" she trailed off, pressing her fingers to her temples. "This is too much."

"I know," he said, his voice raw. "But you need to know something, Alexa. I'm not trying to make your life harder. I just want you to be honest—with James, with me, and with yourself."

She looked up at him, her eyes brimming with tears. "Honesty? That's easy for you to say. You're not the one who could destroy a family with a single choice."

His jaw tightened, but he didn't argue. Instead, he reached out, brushing his hand against her arm. "Do you really think keeping this inside is better? For you? For James? For the kids?"

Her tears spilled over, and she shook her head. "I don't know," she admitted. "I don't know how to make this better without breaking everything."

Jack exhaled deeply, his shoulders slumping. "Alexa, I know this isn't easy. And I'm not asking you to choose me out of guilt or out of obligation. But I need you to hear me when I say this: I'd wait forever if it meant you'd choose me. I said it again."

The words hit her like a tidal wave, and for a moment, she couldn't breathe. There was no anger in his tone, no pressure, just pure, unfiltered longing.

Before she could respond, Jack leaned in, his lips brushing hers in a kiss that wasn't about passion but about longing, about all the years they had spent yearning for what could have been.

When he pulled away, Alexa's breath hitched, her heart pounding in her chest. "Jack…" she began, but the words failed her.

"You don't have to say anything," he said softly. "Not right now."

As Jack stepped back, Alexa felt an overwhelming sense of loss, as if something intangible had been taken from her. He turned and walked down the steps of the porch, his figure disappearing into the darkness.

Alexa stood there for a long time, her emotions a whirlwind of guilt, longing, and confusion. When she finally gathered the strength to return inside, the house was quiet, save for the faint creak of the floorboards beneath her feet.

James was sitting in the living room, his hands clasped tightly around a mug of tea that had long since gone cold. He looked up as Alexa entered, his expression calm but heavy with sadness.

“I was starting to think you weren’t coming back in,” he said quietly.

Alexa hesitated, unsure of what to say. “I just needed some air,” she replied, her voice barely above a whisper.

James nodded, his gaze steady but tired. “I figured.”

Alexa lay awake in bed that night, staring at the ceiling as James slept beside her. His breathing was steady, almost rhythmic, but she could tell he wasn’t truly asleep.

Her mind raced, replaying the events of the evening. She thought about James, about the years they had spent together, the life they had built. She thought about the laughter of their children, the holidays spent around the fireplace, the quiet moments of partnership that had defined their marriage.

And then she thought about Jack—the way he looked at her, the way he spoke to her, the way he kissed her like she was the only person who mattered in the world.

Her chest tightened as she realized that no matter what she chose, someone would be hurt. And there was no way to undo the damage that had already been done.

The next morning, Alexa found herself in the kitchen, preparing breakfast in a haze. Anna walked in, her footsteps light but purposeful.

"Morning, Mom," she said, her tone cautious.

"Morning," Alexa replied, forcing a smile.

Anna leaned against the counter, studying her mother. "Is everything okay?"

Alexa hesitated, her hands freezing over the plate she was preparing. "Why do you ask?"

"I don't know," Anna said, shrugging. "It just seems like something's… different. Between you and Dad."

Alexa's heart sank. She turned to face her daughter, trying to keep her composure. "Your dad and I are just… working through some things," she said carefully.

Anna's brow furrowed, but she nodded. "Okay," she said softly. "I just hope you guys are okay."

Alexa's throat tightened, and she reached out to tuck a strand of hair behind her daughter's ear. "We will be," she said, though she wasn't sure if she believed it.

Meanwhile, James stood on the porch, staring out at the lake. His mind was clearer this morning, though his heart still ached. He thought about Alexa's silence at the dinner table, about the unspoken words that hung between them like a heavy fog.

James had always been a man of action, someone who tackled problems head-on. But this was different. This was something he couldn't fix with a conversation or a gesture. This was something Alexa had to figure out for herself.

And though it pained him to admit it, he knew that pushing her would only drive her further away.

Jack spent the morning walking the trails around the lake, his thoughts as turbulent as the storm that had passed days earlier. He had put everything on the line last night, and now all he could do was wait.

The thought of leaving the Lakehouse and returning to his life in the city felt unbearable. But he knew that staying here, lingering in this limbo, wasn't fair to anyone, least of all Alexa.

By the time he returned to the house, his mind was made up. He would leave, give Alexa the space she needed to figure out what she truly wanted.

Later that afternoon, as the family gathered on the porch for lunch, Jack made his announcement.

"I think it's time for me to head back," he said, his tone casual but his eyes betraying his emotions. James glanced at him, his expression unreadable, while Alexa froze, her fork hovering in midair.

"You don't have to leave yet," Anna said, her voice filled with surprise. "There's still a couple of days before we all head back."

"I know," Jack said, forcing a smile. "But I've got some things to take care of back home."

Alexa looked at him, her heart sinking. She wanted to tell him to stay, but the words wouldn't come.

Later she managed to convince him to stay.

Chapter 11
Goodbye, My Love

The house was silent in the early morning, the kind of stillness that carried the weight of heavy thoughts. Alexa sat in her bedroom, the soft golden light of dawn streaming through the curtains. She hadn't slept. How could she, when the choice she had been avoiding for so long could no longer be postponed?

Her mind raced with memories—of James, steady and devoted, and of Jack, fiery and passionate. Every moment she had spent with either man seemed to flash before her eyes, a kaleidoscope of joy, pain, and longing.

She thought about her children, their laughter filling the house, their innocent trust in her. She thought about James's quiet, unwavering love and how he had been her partner through life's darkest storms. But then, inevitably, her thoughts drifted to Jack—the way he made her feel alive, seen, and understood in ways she hadn't felt in years.

She pressed her hands to her face, the tears spilling over as she whispered to herself, "What do I do?"

The answer came not in a sudden flash but in a slow, steady realization that settled over her like the first rays of sunlight breaking through the dark.

Alexa didn't want to hurt anyone. But no matter what she chose, someone would be hurt. That was the cruel truth of love—it wasn't always fair, and it didn't always come without pain.

Alexa stepped out onto the porch, the crisp morning air biting at her skin. The lake shimmered in the distance, and she found herself drawn to it once again. This place had always been a sanctuary for her, a space where she could think clearly, away from the noise of life.

As she walked the familiar path, she thought about what staying with James truly meant. It wasn't just about choosing the safer option or avoiding guilt was about honoring the life they had built together. He wasn't perfect, but neither was she. And despite the distance that had grown between them, she believed there was still something worth saving.

When she reached the edge of the dock, Alexa stopped, staring out at the water. She closed her eyes and inhaled deeply, letting the stillness seep into her bones.

"I know what I have to do," she whispered, though her voice cracked with emotion.

The decision weighed heavily on Alexa, lingering in every moment she spent in the Lakehouse. That evening, as the kids played a board game in the living room and James sat on the couch reading, Alexa quietly stepped outside onto the porch. The air was cool, the night sky dotted with stars that felt impossibly distant, like the life she once imagined with Jack.

Her heart ached with the finality of her decision, but a sense of calm was beginning to settle over her. She had spent so much of her life running—from her emotions, her desires, her fears—but this time, she was standing still, letting herself face the consequences of her choices.

When Alexa stepped back inside, James looked up, catching the quiet determination in her expression. He closed his book, setting it aside.

"Alexa," he said softly, "can we talk?"

She hesitated but nodded, walking over to sit beside him. The room was dimly lit, the kids' laughter in the background a bittersweet reminder of everything they had built together.

"I know you've been struggling," James began, his voice steady but raw. "And I know I've been blind to it for too long. I just want to say… whatever you decide, I'll understand. I just need to know that you're making the choice that feels right for you. Not for me. Not for anyone else."

For the first time in weeks, James pulled her into his arms, holding her tightly as she cried into his shoulder.

Alexa stood at the edge of the dock, her breath forming soft clouds in the crisp morning air. The lake stretched out before her, calm and reflective, as if it were mirroring the storm that raged inside her. This was the place where so many of her memories with Jack had been made, and now it would be the place where she let him go.

She heard his footsteps before she saw him, the soft crunch of gravel announcing his arrival. She turned, her heart tightening as Jack appeared on the trail, his hands tucked into the pockets of his jacket.

For a moment, they simply looked at each other, the silence between them heavy with everything they wanted to say but couldn't.

"I wasn't sure you'd come," Jack said finally, his voice soft but steady.

Alexa nodded, her throat tight. "I had to."

He stepped closer, his eyes searching hers. "So, this is it, then."

"Alexa," he said softly, his eyes searching hers.

She couldn't hold his gaze, her heart breaking before she even said the words.

"Jack," she began, her voice trembling. "I need to talk to you."

He nodded, stepping closer. "I'm listening."

She nodded again, tears welling in her eyes. "I can't do this anymore, Jack. I can't keep tearing myself apart."

Jack's jaw tightened, but he nodded, his gaze dropping to the ground. "I understand," he said quietly.

Alexa stepped closer, reaching for his hand. Her fingers brushed against his, and he looked up, his eyes filled with a raw vulnerability that broke her heart.

"This doesn't mean I don't love you," she said, her voice trembling. "Because I do. I always will."

"And I'll always love you," Jack replied, his voice breaking. "But I want you to be happy, Alexa. Even if it's not with me."

She closed her eyes, a tear slipped down her cheek. "I hope you find happiness too," she whispered.

Jack cupped her face in his hands, his touch gentle, as if he were afraid, she might shatter. He leaned in, pressing a soft, lingering kiss to her forehead. "You've always been my peace," he said, his voice barely audible.

Alexa's tears came faster now, and she reached up to touch his cheek, her fingers trembling. "You deserve someone who can give you everything, Jack. And I can't. Not now. Not ever."

She swallowed hard, trying to steady herself. "I've made a decision."

His jaw tightened, and he nodded again, though his expression betrayed the hope he was desperately clinging to. "Okay."

"I can't leave James," she said, the words falling from her lips like stones. "I can't break up my family. I can't take that away from the kids. And I can't… I can't walk away from the life we've built together."

Jack's face crumpled, his shoulders sagging as the weight of her words hit him. He looked away, blinking rapidly as if trying to hold back tears.

"I see," he said quietly.

"I'm so sorry," Alexa whispered, her voice thick with emotion.

He turned back to her, his eyes filled with pain but also understanding. "You don't have to apologize, Alexa. I knew this might happen. I just…" He trailed off, struggling to find the words.

"I love you, Jack," she said, her tears spilling over. "I always have. But I can't—"

Their eyes met, and for a moment, the world seemed to stand still. Then, without thinking, Alexa leaned in, her lips meeting his in a kiss that was both tender and desperate. It was a kiss filled with everything they couldn't have a bittersweet goodbye that spoke of love and loss in equal measure.

When they finally pulled apart, Alexa's tears mingled with his, their foreheads resting against each other.

"I know," he interrupted gently, his voice breaking. "I know."

They stood in silence for a long moment, the only sound the gentle lapping of the water against the dock. Then, slowly, Jack reached out and took her hands in his.

"I don't regret any of this," he said, his voice steady despite the tears in his eyes. "Not a single moment. And I'll always love you, Alexa. But I want you to be happy. I want you to find peace."

She nodded, her chest tight with emotion. "I want that for you too," she said softly.

Jack leaned forward, pressing a gentle kiss to her forehead. It wasn't passionate or desperate—it was a goodbye, a promise, and a release all at once.

When he pulled back, he whispered, "If things were different…"

"But they're not," she said, finishing his sentence, her voice heavy with sadness.

"No," he agreed, his tone resigned. "They're not."

"Goodbye, Jack," she whispered, her voice breaking.

"Goodbye, Alexa," he replied, his words heavy with emotion.

Alexa turned and began to walk away, her steps slow and deliberate. Each step felt like a weight pressing down on her chest, but she didn't look back. She couldn't.

Jack watched her go, his hands clenched at his sides, his heart breaking with every step she took. He stayed there long after she disappeared, the stillness of the lake a stark contrast to the turmoil inside him.

Later, across the lake, Jack packed up his belongings, preparing to leave the Lakehouse and the memories it held. He knew it was time to move on, even if it felt like leaving a piece of his heart behind.

As he closed the trunk of his car, he looked back at the lake one last time. The water was calm, the sun setting in a blaze of orange and gold.

"I hope you're happy, Alexa," he murmured, his voice filled with both longing and acceptance.

With that, he got into his car and drove away, leaving the past behind.

When Alexa returned to the Lakehouse, James was in the kitchen, making coffee. He looked up as she walked in, his expression cautious but hopeful.

"Hey," he said softly.

"Hey," she replied, her voice tired but resolute.

James studied her for a moment before stepping closer. "Are you okay?"

Alexa nodded, her eyes meeting his. "I think I will be," she said honestly.

He reached for her hand, his touch warm and steady. "I'm glad you're here," he said, his voice filled with quiet sincerity.

"Me too," she said, a faint smile tugging at her lips.

That evening, Alexa and James sat on the porch, the lake glowing under the soft light of the setting sun. The silence between them was comfortable, a stark contrast to the tension that had filled their relationship in recent weeks.

Alexa went out for a walk, when she returned to the house, James was sitting on the porch, his expression unreadable. He looked up as she approached, his eyes searching hers for answers.

"Did you figure it out?" he asked quietly.

She nodded, her throat tightening. "I did."

"And?"

Alexa stepped closer, her voice trembling as she said, "I choose us, I choose you and our children. I want to stay. I want to make this work. I want us to find our way back to each other."

James's eyes softened, and he stood, closing the distance between them. "Are you sure?" he asked, his voice filled with vulnerability.

"Yes," she said firmly, though tears streamed down her face. "I'm sure."

He pulled her into his arms, holding her tightly as she sobbed against his chest. For the first time in months, Alexa felt a glimmer of hope that they could heal, that they could rebuild, that they could find their way back to the love they once shared.

Early this morning sun poured through the curtains of the Lakehouse, casting a warm glow over Alexa's face as she sat at the small desk in the corner of the bedroom. Her journal lay open before her, its pages filled with years of thoughts, memories, and questions she had never truly answered. Today, she wrote slowly, each word deliberate, her hand trembling as she put pen to paper.

"I've spent so much of my life torn between two worlds. One filled with love, stability, and the family I cherish, and the other with a passion I never thought I'd feel again. Choosing one doesn't mean I don't mourn the other. But today, I must decide who I am, and who I want to be—for myself, for James, for the kids, and even for Jack."

She set the pen down, her chest tightening as she reread her words. Her decision was clear now, though it didn't make the weight of it any easier to bear.

James was in the kitchen, preparing breakfast as the kids lingered in the living room. The smell of bacon and eggs wafted through the air, but Alexa could barely stomach the thought of food.

"Good morning," James said as she entered, his voice cautious but warm.

"Morning," Alexa replied, managing a faint smile.

He glanced at her, his brow furrowed. "You okay?"

"I will be," she said, her voice softer than usual.

James didn't press her. Instead, he turned back to the stove, flipping a pancake with practiced ease. But Alexa could sense the tension radiating from him, the quiet fear he tried so hard to hide.

She sat at the table, watching him. She thought about everything he had given her—his unwavering support, his steady presence, the life they had built together. And she thought about the cracks that had formed between them, the way her heart had wandered even as she clung to the foundation they had laid.

James turned, setting a plate in front of her. "Here," he said, his voice gentle. "Eat something."

"Thank you," she murmured, though she barely touched the food.

That evening, Alexa and James sat together on the couch, their hands intertwined. It was the first time in weeks that they had felt truly connected, and Alexa felt a glimmer of hope.

"I know I've hurt you," Alexa said quietly. "And I know it's going to take time to fix this. But I want to try. I want to make us work."

James squeezed her hand, his gaze steady. "So do I," he said. "But we must be honest with each other—from now on. No more secrets."

"No more secrets," Alexa agreed, her voice firm.

Anna and Luke noticed the change in their parents almost immediately. The tension that had lingered in the house for weeks seemed to lift, replaced by a sense of calm.

"Do you think everything's okay now?" Luke asked his sister one evening.

"I think so," Anna said, a small smile on her face. "They're trying. That's what matters."

For Alexa, the choice to stay wasn't just about James or the kids. It was about choosing stability, choosing the life she had built, and choosing to find happiness within herself.

"We have a lot to work through," Alexa said, breaking the silence. James nodded, his gaze fixed on the horizon. "I know. But I'm willing to try. Are you?"

"Yes," she said firmly. "I want to make this work, James. I want to fight for us." He turned to look at her, his eyes filled with a mix of hope and determination. "Then we'll get through this. Together."

Alexa reached for his hand, lacing her fingers with his. For the first time in a long time, she felt a flicker of hope that maybe, just maybe, they could find their way back to each other. That night, as Alexa lay in bed beside James, her mind drifted to Jack. She thought about his words, his touch, his kiss. She thought about the love they had shared and the sacrifices they had made.

She knew she would always carry a piece of him with her, just as she knew she would always wonder what it might be. But she also knew that she had made the right choice—for herself, for her family, and for the life she wanted to rebuild.

As she drifted off to sleep, Alexa felt a sense of peace she hadn't felt in years. It wasn't perfect, and it wasn't easy, but it was real. And that, she realized, was enough.

In the days and weeks that followed, Alexa and James worked to rebuild their relationship. They took long walks by the lake, shared quiet moments over coffee, and talked about things they hadn't addressed in years.

It wasn't easy—there were still moments of doubt, moments of pain—but they faced them together, determined to move forward.

Jack left the Lakehouse the day after their goodbye, his heart heavy but his resolve strong. He knew it would take time to heal, but he also knew that letting Alexa go was the right thing to do.

He returned to his life, throwing himself into his work and surrounding himself with friends who cared about him. And though the pain lingered, he found comfort in the knowledge that he had done everything he could to fight for the woman he loved.

One day, he hoped he would find peace and the love he deserved..

Chapter 12: A Year Later

The Lakehouse stood just as it always had, nestled among the towering pines, the stillness of the lake reflecting the soft morning light. Alexa sat in the passenger seat, her fingers nervously twisting her wedding ring as James navigated the winding road leading up to the house.

The kids were in the backseat—Anna scrolling through her phone, Luke dozing with his head against the window. The quiet chatter of the radio filled the car, but the atmosphere felt different than it had the year before.

"Looks the same, doesn't it?" James said softly, glancing at Alexa as they approached the driveway.

She nodded, her gaze fixed on the familiar wooden steps leading up to the porch. "Yeah," she replied, though her voice carried the weight of unspoken thoughts.

James reached over and placed his hand on hers. It was a simple gesture, but it meant everything. Alexa looked at him, offering a small, grateful smile.

The year since their last visit had been anything but easy. When they had left the Lakehouse the previous summer, the fractures in their marriage had felt impossible to repair. Alexa had chosen James, but the choice hadn't erased the pain, doubt, and lingering questions.

They had started therapy a month after returning home. It had been James's idea, though Alexa hadn't needed much convincing. Their sessions were raw and often uncomfortable, forcing them to confront years of suppressed feelings and unspoken grievances.

"I felt like I was invisible to you," James had admitted during one session, his voice trembling. "Like I was just… there. A placeholder."

"I didn't mean to make you feel that way," Alexa had said, her tears falling freely. "But I felt invisible too. Like I was just a wife and a mom, and nothing more."

Therapy became their lifeline, a place where they could be honest without fear of judgment. James had confessed his fear of not being enough for her, and Alexa had opened about the ways she had buried her true self for the sake of their family.

It wasn't a magical fix—it never is—but it was a start.

Back at the Lakehouse, Alexa unpacked while James and the kids carried bags up from the car. The air was warm, the scent of pine and fresh water filling the house.

As she arranged clothes in the bedroom, James appeared in the doorway with two mugs of coffee.

"For you," he said, holding one out to her.

She took it with a smile, the simple gesture warming her more than the drink itself. "Thank you."

He leaned against the doorframe, watching her for a moment. "You okay?"

"I think so," she said, meeting his gaze. "It feels… different this time."

"Good different or bad different?"

"Good," she said after a moment, her smile soft but genuine.

That afternoon, Alexa wandered down to the dock while James took the kids into town to pick up groceries. She stood at the edge, staring out at the water, her thoughts drifting to the summer before.

She could almost see Jack sitting there, his feet dangling over the edge, his gaze as steady and intense as ever. The memory was vivid, but it no longer carried the same ache.

She thought about their final goodbye—the way he had held her; the way his voice had trembled when he told her he'd always love her. It had been one of the hardest moments of her life, but she didn't regret it. Letting him go had been the right choice, even if it had broken her heart.

Now, standing on the dock a year later, she felt a strange sense of peace. The love she had shared with Jack would always be a part of her, but it no longer defined her.

The sound of laughter drew Alexa's attention back to the house. She turned to see Anna and Luke running down the trail, their faces flushed with excitement.

"Mom, look!" Anna called, holding up a camera.

Alexa smiled as her daughter bound onto the dock, flipping through the photos she had taken. Anna had discovered a passion for photography earlier that year, and she had been inseparable from her camera ever since.

"These are beautiful," Alexa said, marveling at the way Anna had captured the lake's stillness and the way the sunlight filtered through the trees.

"Thanks," Anna said, beaming.

Luke joined them, holding up a certificate he had earned at his last swim meet. "I got first place," he said proudly.

"That's amazing, Luke!" Alexa said, pulling him into a hug.

As she looked at her children, Alexa felt a renewed sense of purpose. They were her anchor, her reason for everything.

That evening, after the kids had gone to bed, Alexa and James sat on the porch, a bottle of wine between them. The air was cool, the stars scattered across the sky like diamonds.

James reached for her hand, his fingers intertwining with hers. "I missed this," he said softly.

"Me too," Alexa replied, her voice warm.

They sat in comfortable silence for a while, the gentle sounds of the lake filling the space between them.

"You know," James said, breaking the silence, "I was terrified of losing you last year."

Alexa looked at him, her heart tightening. "I was scared too," she admitted.

"But I think we're stronger now," he said, his gaze steady. "Don't you?"

She nodded, her smile genuine. "Yeah, I think we are."

Their marriage wasn't perfect it never would be. They still had disagreements, still stumbled over old wounds and insecurities. But they were learning to navigate those moments with grace and patience, leaning on each other instead of pulling away.

Alexa had learned to speak up when she felt overwhelmed, and James had learned to listen without trying to fix everything. They had rediscovered the small gestures that made their relationship special bringing each other coffee in the morning, holding hands during quiet walks, stealing kisses when the kids weren't looking.

It was in those moments, those imperfect yet beautiful moments, that Alexa felt the depth of their love.

"We're home for the week," James said, reaching for her hand.

"We are," she replied softly, squeezing his hand as they walked toward the house.

As she opened the drawer of the bedside table in her and James's room, she found the notebook she had once used to jot down her thoughts during their last stay. Flipping through its pages, Alexa was struck by how much pain, and confusion filled her words back then.

Now, she felt a quiet sense of pride. She had survived that storm—not just survived, but came through stronger, more self-aware. She had faced her deepest fears and made a decision that allowed her to move forward.

She closed the notebook and tucked it back into the drawer. This week wasn't about dwelling on the past. It was about celebrating the present and the progress they had made.

Later that evening, as the kids played a board game in the living room, Alexa and James sat together on the porch, sipping wine and watching the stars begin to emerge.

"It feels good to be back," Alexa said, her voice calm.

"It does," James replied, glancing at her. "Better than I thought it would."

Alexa turned to him, searching his face. She knew how hard the past year had been for both. The therapy sessions, the late-night arguments, the moments of doubt—it had all been exhausting. But it was also worth it.

"You've been amazing, James," she said softly. "I know I haven't said it enough, but I see how hard you've worked. How much you've fought for us."

James set his glass down and reached for her hand. "I couldn't have done it without you. You were honest, Alexa. Even when it hurt, you told me the truth. That's what saved us."

Tears prickled her eyes, but they were tears of gratitude, not sorrow.

"I'll keep trying," she promised. "Every day."

"So will I," James said, leaning in to kiss her gently.

The next morning, while the kids were still sleeping, Alexa slipped out of the house and made her way to the dock. The lake was serene, its surface like glass, reflecting the sky above.

She sat at the edge, her legs dangling over the water, and let the silence wrap around her. This was where she had spent so many moments with Jack—laughing, talking, sharing pieces of themselves that no one else knew.

The memories were still there, vivid and sharp, but they no longer carried the same ache. Instead, they felt like a chapter in a book part of her story, but not the whole.

"I hope you're doing okay," she murmured, her voice carried away by the gentle breeze. She didn't know where Jack was or what he was doing, but she wished him peace, just as she had found her own.

Anna and Luke came alive during their time at the Lakehouse. Anna's camera was never far from her side, and Alexa loved seeing the world through her daughter's lens.

"Look at this one, Mom," Anna said one afternoon, showing her a shot of the lake at sunset. The colors were breathtaking, the composition perfect.

"It's beautiful," Alexa said, her pride evident. "You've got a real gift, Anna."

Anna beamed. "Thanks. I'm thinking about taking a photography class when school starts."

Alexa nodded. "You absolutely should."

Meanwhile, Luke spent most of his time in the water, practicing his swimming techniques and timing himself on sprints across the lake.

"Mom, did you see that?" he called one afternoon, pulling himself up onto the dock, breathless but grinning.

"I did!" Alexa said, clapping. "You're getting so fast, Luke. Maybe you can join the swim team is next?"

"Maybe," he said, his cheeks flushing with excitement.

These moments reminded Alexa of why she had made the choice to stay. Her children were thriving, their happiness palpable. And that was worth everything.

As the days passed, Alexa and James found small moments to reconnect—sharing coffee on the porch in the early mornings, stealing kisses in the kitchen while the kids weren't looking, taking quiet walks along the trails they had once explored as a young couple.

During one such walk, James reached for her hand, his grip warm and reassuring.

"You know," he said, his tone thoughtful, "I was worried for a long time that we'd never get back to this."

"Back to what?" Alexa asked, her voice curious.

"This," he said, gesturing to the trail ahead. "The simplicity. Just us, together. No walls, no secrets. Just us."

Alexa smiled, her heart swelling. "I was worried about that too," she admitted. "But I think we've found it again. Or at least, we're finding it."

James stopped walking and turned to her, his hands resting on her shoulders. "I'm proud of us, Alexa," he said sincerely. "We've come a long way."

"So am I," she said, leaning in to kiss him.

Another day, Alexa ventured down to the old boathouse; a place she had avoided all week. It was where she and Jack had shared some of their most intimate moments, and the thought of facing those memories had felt daunting.

But now, standing in the doorway, she realized she was ready.

The boathouse was just as she remembered it, its walls lined with old fishing gear and faded photographs. She ran her fingers over the wooden beams, her heart aching but steady.

"This was never going to be easy," she murmured to herself. "But it was necessary."

She stood there for a while, letting the memories wash her. When she finally left, she felt lighter, as if she had left a part of her pain behind.

That night, the family gathered on the porch to watch the sunset, their laughter mingling with the sounds of the lake. Anna snapped photos of the sky, while Luke made jokes that had everyone in stitches.

James wrapped an arm around Alexa, pulling her close. "This feels right," he said softly.

"It does," Alexa agreed, her head resting on his shoulder.

As the sun dipped below the horizon, casting the lake in hues of gold and orange, Alexa felt a sense of peace she hadn't known for years.

This wasn't a perfect ending. Life was rarely perfect. But it was hers, and for the first time in a long time, she felt like she was exactly where she was meant to be.

Alexa and James sat on the porch, the moonlight casting a soft glow over the lake. They shared a bottle of wine, the silence between them comfortable for the first time in what felt like years.

"Do you ever think about last summer?" James asked, breaking the quiet.

Alexa turned to look at him, her heart tightening slightly. "I do," she admitted. "But not in the way I used to."

He nodded, taking a sip of his wine. "I think about it too," he said. "But I don't think we'd be here if it hadn't happened."

"I know we wouldn't," Alexa said softly.

Their work to rebuild their marriage over the past year had been grueling. It wasn't easy, but it was worth it. They weren't perfect—far from it—but they were trying. And that mattered.

Alexa rose early, slipping out of bed while the rest of the house still slept. She made her way down to the dock, the cool morning air brushing against her skin.

Sitting on the edge, she let her feet dangle over the water, her thoughts drifting to Jack. She hadn't spoken to him since the day they said goodbye, and though she missed him, the pain of his absence had dulled.

She thought about the way he had looked at her that day, his eyes filled with both love and sorrow. *"I'll always love you, but I hope you find peace,"* he had said.

And she had.

The memories of their time together were no longer a source of regret. They were a part of her story, a chapter that had shaped her but no longer defined her.

Later that day, Alexa watched as Anna crouched by the edge of the lake, her camera clicking as she captured the sunlight filtering through the trees.

"You're really getting good at this," Alexa said, kneeling beside her.

Anna beamed. "Thanks, Mom. I think I want to do something with photography when I get older."

Alexa felt a swell of pride. "You can do anything you set your mind to," she said, brushing a strand of hair from Anna's face.

Nearby, Luke was practicing his swimming, his strokes strong and confident. James stood at the end of the dock, cheering him on, his voice filled with enthusiasm.

Watching her family, Alexa felt a deep sense of gratitude for the life they had built together. It wasn't perfect, but it was theirs.

That evening, as they sat around the dinner table, James reached for Alexa's hand, his touch warm and grounding. She looked at him, surprised, and he gave her a small smile.

"I just wanted to say thank you," he said, his voice steady.

"For what?" Alexa asked, her brow furrowing.

"For staying," he said simply. "For choosing us."

Her throat tightened, and she squeezed his hand. "I don't regret it," she said, her voice barely above a whisper.

As the kids played down by the water, Alexa ventured along the old forest trail that looped around the lake. The crunch of leaves beneath her shoes and the soft rustle of the wind in the trees brought a wave of nostalgia. This was the path she had walked so many times as a child, as a teenager, and even last year with Jack.

She paused when she reached a familiar clearing—the spot where she and Jack had often met during those long-ago summers. The memories came rushing back: their laughter, their whispered dreams for the future, the way they would sit side by side, skipping stones across the lake's surface.

The ache in her chest was gentler now, not as sharp as it had been a year ago. The weight of regret had lifted, replaced by a quiet understanding of the choices she had made. She would always cherish what she and Jack had shared, but it no longer felt like a loss. It felt like a part of her story, one that had shaped her but didn't define her.

Back at the Lakehouse, Alexa found Anna sitting on the porch, with her camera in hand. The teenager's brow was furrowed in concentration as she adjusted the lens, aiming it at the vibrant foliage across the lake.

"Whitcher working on?" Alexa asked, sitting down beside her.

Anna lowered the camera and smiled. "Just trying to get the right angle. The light's perfect right now."

Alexa leaned closer, peeking at the photo Anna had just taken. The image was stunning—an interplay of light and shadow that perfectly captured the serene beauty of the lake.

"You've got quite the eye," Alexa said, pride swelling in her chest.

"Thanks," Anna replied, her cheeks flushing with a mix of pride and embarrassment. "I'm thinking about submitting some of my photos to the school art show this year."

"You absolutely should," Alexa said, squeezing her daughter's shoulder. "You're so talented, Anna. I'm proud of you."

Anna beamed, and Alexa couldn't help but feel a deep sense of gratitude for moments like this.

Later that afternoon, Luke proudly showed off his swimming skills, diving effortlessly into the lake and cutting through the water with practiced strokes. Alexa and James stood on the dock, watching as he reached the floating platform in the middle of the lake.

"Mom! Dad! Did you see that?" Luke called, his face shining with excitement.

"We saw!" James called back, clapping his hands. "You've been working hard, buddy. It shows."

Alexa smiled as she watched James cheer for their son, the pride evident in his voice. Moments like this reminded her why she had chosen to stay, to rebuild what they had.

That evening, after the kids had gone to bed, Alexa and James sat together on the porch, sipping wine and watching the moonlight ripple across the lake. The silence between them was comfortable now, no longer weighed down by unspoken resentment.

James reached for her hand, his fingers intertwining with hers. "Thanks for coming back here," he said softly.

Alexa turned to look at him, her heart swelling with affection. "It feels different this time," she admitted.

"Good different?" he asked, his lips quirking into a small smile.

She nodded. "Good different."

As they sat there, hand in hand, Alexa felt a sense of peace she hadn't known in a long time. Their journey was far from over, but for the first time, she felt like they were truly on the same path.

On their last day at the Lakehouse, Alexa took a solo walk along the trails she and Jack had explored as kids. The sunlight filtered through the trees, casting dappled patterns on the ground.

She paused at a familiar spot, a clearing overlooking the lake where she and Jack had once sat for hours, talking about their dreams for the future.

"I hope you've found peace," she whispered, her voice carried away by the breeze.

She stood there for a moment longer before turning back toward the house, her heart lighter than it had been in a long time.

That evening, as the sun set over the lake, James set up a tripod to take a family photo. Anna rolled her eyes but couldn't hide her smile as Luke tried to pose like a superhero.

"Alright, everyone," James said, setting the timer. "Smile!"

Alexa stood between her children, her hand resting on James's shoulder. As the camera clicked, she felt a surge of gratitude for the life they had rebuilt together. It wasn't perfect, but it was theirs.

As they packed up the car the next morning, Alexa took one last look at the Lakehouse. The memories of the past still lingered, but they no longer held her captive.

She slid into the passenger seat, glancing at James as he started the car. He reached over and took her hand, his grip warm and steady. "Ready?" he asked. "Ready," she said, her smile reflecting the quiet confidence she felt. As they drove away, Alexa looked out at the lake one last time. It was a place of beginnings and endings, of love and loss. But most importantly, it was a place that had helped her find herself again.

Chapter 13

The Lake's Memory

The lake stretched out before Alexa, still and reflective, its surface catching the pale light of dawn. The air was crisp, carrying the faint scent of pine and wet earth, grounding her in the moment. She stood at the edge of the dock, barefoot, the cool wood beneath her feet, a reminder of all the summers she had spent here.

This time, she was alone. The children were with James, who had encouraged her to take the day for herself. "Go," he had said, his voice soft but sure. "You need this."

And so here she was, at the lake that had shaped her, that had witnessed her greatest joys and deepest heartbreaks. The water rippled slightly in the breeze, as if whispering secrets from its depths. Alexa closed her eyes, letting the sounds and smells of the lake wash over her.

Alexa opened her eyes and sat down on the edge of the dock, letting her legs dangle over the water. The lake had always felt like a mirror, reflecting not just the world around it but the state of her soul.

She thought back to all the phases of her life that had played out here. As a child, the lake had been a place of innocence—a playground where she and Jack had raced each other to the shore and skipped stones until their arms ached.

As a teenager, the lake had taken on a new meaning, becoming a backdrop for late-night conversations and stolen glances with Jack. It had been a place of unspoken promises and emotions too big for words.

And then, as an adult, the lake had become something else entirely: a witness to her struggles, her betrayals, and ultimately, her choices.

Now, sitting here alone, she saw the lake for what it truly was—a constant, unchanging presence in her ever-shifting life.

Her thoughts inevitably drifted to Jack, as they always did when she was here. She could still see him so clearly, standing on the dock beside her, his eyes filled with a mix of longing and determination.

"If you stay, I'll let you go. But if you leave, I'll be waiting."

The words had haunted her for months after that day, replaying in her mind as she wrestled with her decision. She had chosen James, but she had never stopped wondering what might have been.

Now, a year later, the ache of that decision had softened. The sharp edges of her longing had dulled, replaced by a bittersweet understanding. Jack had been her first love, her deepest connection, but their story had always been one of the missed opportunities and impossible choices.

She closed her eyes, letting the memories wash over her. She thought of his smile, his laugh, the way he had looked at her as if she were the only person in the world.

"I hope you're happy," she whispered, her voice barely audible over the gentle lapping of the water.

Alexa leaned back on her hands, staring up at the sky. Her thoughts turned to her mother, Bridgette, whose presence still lingered in the Lakehouse and in Alexa's heart.

Growing up, Bridgette had always seemed larger than life—sharp, confident, and unyielding. But as Alexa had read through her mother's letters and pieced together the fragments of her past, she had come to see Bridgette as something else: human.

Bridgette had struggled with love and fidelity, just as Alexa had. She had made mistakes, wrestled with guilt, and carried the weight of choices that couldn't be undone.

But Bridgette's life hadn't been a cautionary tale, Alexa realized now. It had been a lesson. Her mother's flaws and struggles weren't meant to be a blueprint for Alexa to follow but a reminder that life was messy, that love was complicated, and that no one had all the answers.

"Thank you," Alexa murmured, her voice catching. "For everything."

As the sun climbed higher in the sky, Alexa thought about James and the life they had built together. Choosing him wasn't easy—it had taken months of therapy, countless late-night conversations, and a willingness to confront the cracks in their marriage.

But they had done it. They had rebuilt something fragile yet strong, imperfect yet beautiful.

She thought about the small moments that had brought them back together, James surprising her with coffee in the mornings, reaching for her hand during a quiet walk, or making her laugh with his silly impressions. These gestures weren't grand or sweeping, but they were real.

For the first time in years, Alexa felt like she could breathe again.

And yet, even as she felt at peace with her choice, Alexa knew she would always carry Jack with her. He had been a part of her for so long, his presence woven into the fabric of her life.

But loving Jack didn't mean she had to be with him. She understood that now. Love wasn't always about possession or permanence, it was about connection, about the way someone could shape your heart and your soul, even from afar.

"I'll always love you," she whispered to the lake, her voice steady. "But I need to let you go."

The words felt like a release, a final goodbye to the man who had meant so much to her.

As the morning stretched into afternoon, Alexa felt a sense of calm settle over her. The lake had always been her sanctuary, and now it felt like a place of healing.

She stood, brushing off her jeans, and took one last look at the water. The lake would always hold her memories, but it no longer felt like a burden.

"Thank you," she said softly, her words carried away by the breeze.

The trees lining the road swayed gently in the late afternoon breeze, their branches bending as if to welcome her back. The memories came rushing in—the laughter of her children, the quiet dinners on the porch, the stolen moments with Jack that had changed her life forever.

Inside, the house smelled faintly of cedar and rain. Dust motes floated in the sunlight streaming through the windows. Alexa dropped her bag near the couch and took a slow walk through the house.

She lingered in the kitchen, running her fingers along the counter where she had shared quiet mornings with James and late-night conversations with Jack. She touched the back of one of the dining chairs, remembering the tension-filled family dinner where James had first confronted her.

It felt like a lifetime ago.

Upstairs, Alexa found herself in the attic, where Bridgette's letters still rested in a small box. She hadn't opened them since that summer, but now she felt ready.

Alexa sat cross-legged on the wooden floor and pulled out one of the letters. Bridgette's handwriting, sharp and precise, danced across the page:

"Alexa, life is not about the choices you avoid but the ones you face head-on. Regret comes from indecision, not from making mistakes."

The words hit her like a wave. For so long, she had been paralyzed by fear of making the wrong choice. But now, as she sat in the attic of her childhood, she realized she had made peace with her decisions.

The next morning, Alexa woke up before sunrise. She brewed a cup of coffee and carried it down to the dock, the wooden boards creaking softly under her weight. The air was cool and damp, and the lake was perfectly still, its surface reflecting the soft hues of dawn.

She sat on the edge of the dock, her feet just above the water, and sipped her coffee in silence.

The lake had always been a place of clarity for her. It held so many of her memories—good and bad. Summers spent swimming with Jack, the excitement of teaching her children to paddle a canoe, the stormy night when she and Jack had kissed for the first time.

Now, as she looked out at the water, she saw the lake not as a symbol of turmoil but of resilience. It had weathered countless storms, yet it always returned to its natural state of calm.

As the sun rose, painting the sky with shades of pink and gold, Alexa found herself speaking aloud.

"I hope you're happy, Jack," she whispered, her voice carried by the gentle breeze.

She closed her eyes, picturing him somewhere far away. Maybe he was walking along a city street or sitting at his drafting table, designing another masterpiece. Wherever he was, she hoped he had found the peace she had wished for him that summer.

The ache in her chest was still there, but it was softer now, less raw. Loving Jack had changed her but letting him go had allowed her to grow.

Alexa reached into her jacket pocket and pulled out another one of Bridgette's letters, the edges worn from years of being folded and unfolded. She read it aloud, her voice breaking slightly as she spoke the words:

"Alexa, love is messy. It doesn't fit neatly into boxes, and it rarely goes as planned. But it's worth it. Even the heartbreak. Because love is what makes life bearable. It's what gives it meaning."

For so long, she had been angry with her mother, resenting the choices Bridgette had made. But now, sitting by the lake, Alexa understood. Bridgette had been human, flawed but trying her best. Just like Alexa was.

"I forgive you, Mom," Alexa said softly, folding the letter and tucking it back into her pocket.

Alexa walked slowly toward the dock, her footsteps unhurried. She paused at the edge of the water, staring into the rippling surface. The lake, with its endless depths, felt like an extension of her own soul—holding her secrets, her pain, and her moments of clarity.

The stillness of the water reminded her of the quiet moments in her life, the times when she had felt at peace. The storms that occasionally swept across the surface mirrored the chaos she had endured—her conflicts with

James, the emotional upheaval Jack had brought, and the inner turmoil of choosing between love and duty.

Alexa crouched down, dipping her fingers into the cool water. The sensation was grounding, a reminder that while life had its turbulence, there were moments of calm to be found in its aftermath.

As Alexa sat on the dock, watching the sun sink lower in the sky, her thoughts inevitably turned to Jack. She wondered where he was, what his life looked like now. Did he think of her as often as she thought of him? Did he regret what they had shared, or was he at peace with how it had ended?

She imagined him far away, perhaps in a city surrounded by the architecture he loved, his hands sketching plans for some beautiful new structure. Alexa smiled faintly at the thought, though her chest ached with the bittersweetness of it all.

"I hope you're happy," she whispered, her voice carried away by the soft breeze.

She thought about their last moment together by the lake, the way he had kissed her one final time, his words still echoing in her mind: *"I'll always love you, but I hope you find peace."*

And she had. Slowly, piece by piece, Alexa had begun to rebuild her life—not as the woman Jack had loved, nor as the perfect wife James had once envisioned, but as herself.

Alexa leaned back on her hands, her gaze shifting to the trees that lined the edge of the property. Somewhere among them was the attic where she had discovered her mother's letters, the revelations about Bridgette's own struggles with love and fidelity.

For years, Alexa had viewed her mother through a narrow lens—sharp, controlling, emotionally distant. But the letters had revealed a different side of Bridgette, one that Alexa had never truly understood until now.

Bridgette's life had been filled with contradictions, her choices often shaped by a fear of losing control. Alexa now saw that her mother's infidelity and the sharp advice she had given her daughter about love weren't meant to define Alexa's life but to warn her of the dangers of denying her true self.

"You weren't perfect," Alexa murmured, her voice soft, "but I get it now. You were just trying to figure it out, like the rest of us."

For the first time, she felt a sense of forgiveness—not just for Bridgette, but for herself.

As the sky darkened and the first stars appeared, Alexa reflected on the love she had carried for both James and Jack. It wasn't as simple as choosing one over the other; it never had been. Love, she realized, wasn't about possession or permanence. It was about connection, growth, and acceptance.

James had been her foundation, the man who stood beside her through life's storms. He had taught her the value of stability, of showing up even when it was hard. Their marriage wasn't perfect, but it was real, and it was worth fighting for.

Jack, on the other hand, had been the spark, the reminder that passion and longing were just as vital as stability. He had shown her parts of herself she had forgotten, reigniting a fire that had long been smothered by routine.

Both men had shaped her, challenged her, and forced her to confront the truths she had buried deep within.

"I loved you both," Alexa whispered, her voice breaking. "In different ways. For different reasons."

But the weight of that love no longer felt like a burden. It was simply part of her story.

As the hours passed, Alexa felt a sense of peace settled over her. The lake, the dock, the memories—they no longer felt like chains holding her back. Instead, they felt like a part of her foundation, something she could carry forward with grace.

She stood, brushing off her hands and taking one last look at the water. The stars reflected on the surface, their light shimmering like fragments of the past.

Alexa took a deep breath, her shoulders relaxing as she turned to walk back toward the Lakehouse. She didn't know what the future would hold, but for the first time in a long time, she felt ready to face it.

Before leaving the lake, Alexa stopped by the old wooden swing that hung from the large oak tree near the house. She had spent countless summers on that swing as a child, her laughter echoing through the air.

She sat down, her hands gripping the worn ropes, and closed her eyes. She let the gentle motion of the swing soothe her, her mind drifting between past and present.

When she opened her eyes, the moon was high in the sky, its light illuminating the Lakehouse. It felt like a symbol of the life she had chosen—the imperfections, the challenges, and the beauty of it all.

Later that afternoon, Alexa heard the familiar crunch of gravel in the driveway. She stepped onto the porch to see James's car pulling in. He climbed out, holding a small bouquet of wildflowers he had picked along the way.

"You didn't think I'd let you come up here alone, did you?" he said with a small smile.

Alexa felt a warmth spread through her chest. James had changed over the past year, as had she. Their marriage wasn't perfect, it probably never would be—but they were learning to meet each other halfway.

"Thank you for coming," she said, stepping forward to take the flowers.

"Always," James replied, his hand brushing hers.

They spent the rest of the evening walking along the trails by the lake, the silence between them comfortable. When they reached the dock, James pulled her close, pressing a kiss on her forehead.

"You, okay?" he asked.

"I am," Alexa said, her voice steady. And for the first time in a long time, she meant it.

As the weekend went on, Alexa and James were joined by Anna and Luke, who arrived excited to revisit their favorite childhood spots. Anna had brought her camera, snapping pictures of everything from the lake to the wildflowers blooming along the trails.

"Mom, come look at this!" she called, showing Alexa a photo of the sunrise over the lake.

"It's beautiful," Alexa said, her heart swelling with pride.

Luke spent most of his time swimming, his laughter echoing across the water. Watching her children thrive reminded Alexa of why she had made the choices she had made.

Her family wasn't perfect, but it was hers.

Later that evening, as the family sat around the dinner table, Alexa felt a sense of contentment she hadn't felt in years. The laughter of her children, the warmth of James's hand resting lightly on hers—it all felt like enough.

For the first time in a long time, Alexa wasn't looking back. She wasn't questioning her choices or longing for what might have been.

She was here, at this moment, with the people she loved. And that was all she needed.

Before heading to bed, Alexa stepped out onto the porch, the cool night air brushing against her skin. She looked out at the lake, its surface glimmering under the moonlight.

The lake had been a witness to her life, its storms, its depths. It held her memories, her joys, her regrets. But it also held her strength, her resilience, and her ability to move forward.

"I'm ready," she said softly, the words a promise to herself.

And as she turned to go inside, Alexa smiled, her heart light and her steps steady.

On their final morning at the lake, Alexa woke early again and walked down to the dock. This time, James joined her, carrying two cups of coffee.

They sat together in silence, the rising sun casting a golden glow over the water.

"You've been quiet this weekend," James said finally, his tone gentle.

"Just thinking," Alexa replied, her voice soft.

"About?"

"Everything," she said with a small smile. "The past. The future. Us."

James nodded, taking a sip of his coffee. "And?"

"And I think we're going to be okay," Alexa said, her hand finding his.

James squeezed her hand, his gaze steady. "I think so too."

As they packed up to leave, Alexa took one last walk around the lake, letting the memories wash over her. She thought about the girl she had been, the woman she had become, and the journey that had brought her here.

She didn't know what the future held, but for the first time in years, she felt at peace with the choices she had made.

When they drove away from the Lakehouse, Alexa glanced back one last time, the house and the water disappearing behind the trees.

It wasn't goodbye—it never would be.

REVIEWS ARE WELCOME

www.ingramcontent.com/pod-product-compliance
Lightning Source LLC
LaVergne TN
LVHW022201200926
848481LV00006B/1807